BETWEEN
URBAN and WILD

A BUR OAK BOOK

Holly Carver, series editor

BETWEEN
URBAN and WILD

Reflections from Colorado

———

ANDREA M. JONES

University of Iowa Press
Iowa City

University of Iowa Press, Iowa City 52242
Copyright © 2013 by Andrea M. Jones
www.uiowapress.org
Printed in the United States of America

Design by Omega Clay

The University of Iowa Press is a member of Green Press Initiative
and is committed to preserving natural resources.

Printed on acid-free paper

LCCN: 2013933618
ISBN-13: 978-1-60938-187-5
ISBN-10: 1-60938-187-4

This one's for you, Dad.

CONTENTS

The View from Home . . . 1

Voyeur . . . 14

First Signs . . . 22

Lay of the Land . . . 25

Where Does Your Garden Grow? . . . 39

Five Ways of Seeing a Mountain Lion . . . 42

Love Letter to a Sewage Lagoon . . . 47

Reaping an Unexpected Harvest . . . 53

A Walk in the Park . . . 57

Modern Frontier . . . 77

Tyranny of the Visible . . . 84

Contemplating the Fire Seasons . . . 99

Weed Duty . . . 103

Horse Lessons . . . 109

Picking Up the Unexpected . . . 131

Winter Outlook . . . 134

Fourmile Postscript . . . 142

A Day with Nothing More Urgent than This . . . 158

Return . . . 161

My Life as a Weed . . . 175

Acknowledgments . . . 185

BETWEEN
URBAN and WILD

The View from Home

You might say it started with the bird feeder.

Oh, sure, first there was the guy, the falling in love, the settling down in a house in the Colorado foothills. But where the bird feeder enters my memory, a different point of view asserts itself. Not a complete revolution in seeing, but a shift in perspective, as if someone had clapped their hands around my skull and swiveled my head, sighting it along a new angle, saying, "*There*. Try looking there."

I had admired the flickering, fluttering, swooping activity around the feeders at the house of one of our new neighbors. They had a *lot* of bird feeders—tube feeders, wire cages for vegetarian suet, mesh bags filled with peanuts, platform feeders, spikes with dried ears of corn stuck on them. They even had a little wooden box with a flip-up lid, mounted at a level that made it easy for the squirrels and deer to help themselves. It was all too much for me; birds flew in and out with patternless frenetic energy, and trying to keep so many contraptions filled was, I knew, far beyond the limits of my enthusiasm and patience.

One feeder, though: I liked that idea. A point of focus outside the window of my office, something to stare at when my mental moorings broke loose and my mind went adrift.

I bought a basic tube feeder, a clear plastic hexagon ringed with two tiers of feeding ports, and a small bag of mixed birdseed. I put the feeder up on a dead stub jutting from one of the many ponderosa pines on the slope on the west side of the house, outside my office window.

A bird or two might have flown in for seed before the raccoons found the feeder, but I'm not certain. In any case, one of the three waddling bandits pulled the feeder off the branch the first night, and the family dined extravagantly. We turned on the exterior lights when we heard the clunking outside and settled down to watch. The raccoons glanced indifferently toward our faces in the window now and again as they ate.

The feeder was empty but unharmed, and the next day we stretched wire between two trees and suspended the feeder in the middle. The raccoons were unwilling to venture out onto this tightrope, but the squirrels were entirely at home with the arrangement. They took about a day to empty the feeder, instead of accomplishing the job in one fell thump. I added a baffle, a cone of metal that acted like an umbrella, sheltering the feeder from the rain of squirrels from above, and it finally became the domain of the winged.

Fluttering on and off the perches in quick sorties, the birds obliged my expectations. There was something reassuring about seeing their movements when I glanced up from my desk. Often, my eyes were on the birds while my mind was elsewhere, but I watched at times with full attention. Patterns began to emerge. Certain types of birds would fly up to the feeder, grab a seed, and swoop to a nearby tree to hammer the prize into a cranny in the bark. Others settled on the perches for a few minutes at a time, pecking daintily. Some swept showers of millet onto the ground, hunting for the prize of a sunflower seed. Five or six different species used the feeder. I could make distinctions among the plumages, but I didn't know the names of the birds I was looking at.

. . .

Watching the activity around the bird feeder, I realized that my acquaintance with evergreen landscapes had been rather selective, despite the fact that our family headed for the hills, for evergreen forests, for lakes and rivers during my parents' free time. These habits persisted after Mom and Dad split up, with Cindy, Dad's longtime girlfriend and my second mom, embracing the customs. As a result, family vacation memories, for me, do not involve ball games or cross-country drives, amusement parks or museums, cities or Disney glitz. Most of my recollections of our leisure hours together involve evening fishing trips, long weekends camping, days in the woods cutting firewood or hunting for Christmas trees, and Sunday drives (no matter what day of the week) that consisted of meandering slowly along gravel and dirt roads, stopping to peer at deer and elk through binoculars. The perceptual training of these experiences has stuck; my eyes instinctively search for the tawny shapes and white butts of deer, elk, pronghorn, bighorn sheep. I know what the fish common to southwestern Colorado look and taste like, know when to keep my eyes peeled for chokecherries, wild strawberries, and raspberries. The smell of pine woods on a hot day, the springy feel of the litter of needles and cone fragments under a spruce tree, the cartoon-chatter scolding of red squirrels, the lusty wail of an elk's bugle—all are familiar and reassuring.

But as the birds arrived at the feeder with a purr of wing-beats, I realized that they were, for all practical purposes, a new form of fauna to my eyes. I had never paid any attention to small birds before, had never thought of them as wildlife.

I could identify the most common or noisy or charismatic species, such as robins, magpies, hummingbirds, and gray jays. In the classification scheme I inherited from my father, though, songbirds were neither game animals nor varmints. They were, literally, background noise.

Seeking to fill some of the gaps in my knowledge of this novel category of wildlife, I bought a field guide. Consulting its photos and text, I began to put names to the nameless: white-breasted, red-breasted, and pygmy nuthatches; mountain and black-capped chickadees. These, along with juncos in both pink-sided and Oregon forms, made up the majority of the feeder's visitors. Electric blue Steller's jays occasionally flew in as gangs of three or more and acted like loitering teenagers: flashy, loud, eating more than was seemly. With my eyes tuned in to seeing small birds, I began keeping the field guide out where I could consult its pages even when not sitting in my office chair. As they were added to the small mental list of birds I could identify on sight, the species names also made their way into my vocabulary: hairy woodpecker, western tanager, mourning dove, canyon wren, brown creeper, violet-green swallow.

My scant knowledge of biblical lore suggests that naming the beasts gave Adam dominion over them. I had no such designs, but the names were surprisingly empowering. Although they contributed mere syllables to what I knew about the birds, the names acted as keys, unlocking access to a store of information I'd never tapped before. Noticing these birds, then labeling them and finding something out about their lifeways that I did not learn from my own observations altered the quality of my attention. The habit of identifying unknown birds helped knit observations of my environment to my propensity for book-learning.

This all sounds childishly simple, I know, a pitiful example of delayed development. Consulting texts is one of the tried-

and-true ways we modern humans learn about the world. But for me, before this, natural history was an embodied pursuit rather than an intellectual one. I much enjoyed the simple pleasure of seeing, smelling, hearing, touching, occasionally tasting. Encounters with wild animals and natural beauty were sensory trinkets I gathered like shells in a jar, pulled out and admired now and again but neither arranged with much care nor integrated with everyday experience. Bending down to examine a flower, catching sight of the ashy flash of fur as a gray fox disappeared into the underbrush: these were passing interludes, standalone events.

I had moved to the house on Fourmile Canyon Drive with Doug, who would become my husband a couple of years later. I'd recently quit my job and started taking graduate courses through a distance-learning university while working on freelance writing and editing projects. The house was nestled in a rocky gulch in the foothills a few miles west of Boulder, Colorado, surrounded by ponderosa pines. Instead of commanding views over the town and the plains spilling beyond, the windows looked out on nearby slopes crowded with evergreens and spotted with outcrops of pink granite. The neighboring houses were above us, well screened by pine trees. The location felt intimate, compact and accessible. The double shift, to a new home and away from the cubicle work routine, made me feel a bit like one of those people who packs up and moves to a foreign country. I didn't have the resources or gumption to journey to Tuscany or Provence, but I was in a new place with the opportunity to cultivate an altered daily groove. The changes knocked my perspective askew just enough to bring an awareness of my place in the wider world into sharper relief.

As a stay-at-home non-mom, I had the leisure to explore and the inclination to reflect, and I became present on my new home ground in a way I'd never been before. The woodland setting felt comfortable and familiar, but living full time in a setting more wild than suburban was quite different from relaxing during a weekend camping trip. Events in the exterior environment weren't everyday in the sense of being commonplace, yet they became a fixture of my experience every day. The interval between routine and remarkable shrank. Brief sightings and small details accrued into a mosaic, each small observational event a fragment contributing dimension and subtlety to a larger whole. Within the outline of terrain and trees, I pieced in facets of animals and plants, scents and sounds. The house buffered the weather and delineated our territory from that of the critters, true enough, but over time I was able to track the mood of my surroundings through sunlight, rain, and snow; through seasonal shifts of light; through wet years and dry ones. The birds outside my office window started out as a visual diversion, but they metamorphosed into fluttering invitations to learn more about the natural community into which I had moved.

. . .

My father shaped my early understanding about the relationship between people and the natural world. His father was a timberman whose children grew up logging and working in the small family-run sawmill in Colorado's Wet Mountains. Dad later worked for the Job Corps and the U.S. Forest Service in the San Juan Mountains of southwestern Colorado, so from his boyhood through his young adult career, he worked in the woods. Knowledge of trees and natural history were part of his upbringing and his early professional life, but he was also a lifelong fisherman and hunter, which meant that the outdoors was also the setting for most of his favorite pastimes and an outlet for his skills. There's no question, too, that the natural world was as close to a house of worship as any place could be for him, a space for reflection and renewal. Dad was simultaneously pragmatic and reverential about the woods: they supplied meat and lumber, solitude and beauty.

I didn't exactly grow up in town, but my childhood was more suburban than my dad's. The two homes outside of Durango, Colorado, where we lived when I was young were set in a patchwork of agricultural land and ad hoc developments scattered through piñon scrubland. My three older brothers and I spent more of our free time outside than inside, but the landscapes we roamed were more managed than wild. Our landmarks were gravel roads, fences, yards, and septic ponds, not just gullies, trees, and hills.

I have no doubt that my father was a wealth of knowledge about the outdoors, although much of what he understood about the woods was probably so deeply embedded in his mind and experience that he didn't recognize it as acquired knowledge. I think he expected us kids to watch and learn, assuming that we would pick up essential nuggets by way of observation. This seems to have worked to a certain extent; I feel confident being outside and have learned some practical skills, such as how to put on tire chains, although I have no memory of being taught this. But I also lack memories of fatherly counsel about the names of things or the relationships among animals and plants and the land that we would these days label forest ecology. When my dad did choose to be pedantic, his topics were either highly practical or more philosophical: he taught me how to thoroughly douse a campfire, the necessity of getting my camp bed made before dark, and that I shouldn't count on anyone but myself to look out for my safety and well-being.

Thinking back, I can't shake the sense that I missed out on much of what he knew about wildland environments. Perhaps I asked questions when I was younger and then forgot what he said. I might have gotten shorted; as the youngest of four kids I might have been told to go ask one of my brothers when I pestered Dad with questions. Other than accompanying him a few times to pack out meat, I never went hunting, and there's no question that I did not receive many of the insights that he passed on to my two eldest brothers when he taught them to hunt and handle guns. My gender would not have been a barrier—he would have been thrilled to have his daughter hunt with him, I think—but I had no interest in hunting or shooting, and since I was a girl there was no presumption that I *needed* to learn those things.

A more comprehensive inheritance was also blocked because I am nothing like my father in terms of sociability. My dad loved bullshitting with people, whether family members, work colleagues, or barflys. I'm not that social; I take after my mom in being more solitary and thanks to her am an avid reader: I'm content to find out what people have to say by way of the crafted and filtered mechanism of written language. Dad and I once had a terrific screaming fight in the parking lot of a bar. I had retreated to the pickup, preferring solitude and a book to the night's festivities. Such behavior was acceptable when I was a child, but I had recently graduated from high school and was on the cusp of adulthood. In his mind, that meant conducting relationships in an adult fashion, which included negotiating the crowds of bars and taverns. He mistook my shyness and dislike of smoke and noise for snobbery and was furious that I wasn't inside rubbing shoulders with real people with real-life experiences.

What my dad was missing in that long-ago argument was that books are written by real people with real-life experiences, but with the advantage of hindsight I can see additional forces lurking behind our disagreement. Partly, we were screaming across a generation gap, but we were also shouting from acutely offset angles at a sharp bend in the cultural highway. The men and women who had raised and mentored him—and he himself—weren't bookish sorts. Knowledge came from experience, including the experience of elders and compatriots. He understood the advantages of the alternate path of formal learning, as indicated by his insistence that I go to college and not ride horses for a living, but he also recognized what might be lost if I didn't maintain ties to people more literally grounded.

One of the implications of that underlying conflict can be seen in my move with Doug to the house in Fourmile Canyon and, later, to Cap Rock Ranch. Like thousands, if not millions, of people, Doug and I headed for the hills in search of seclusion and space. Having arrived on what was in many respects foreign ground, I found myself wanting to seek advice. The field guides helped fill in some of the factual blanks about flora and fauna, but they could not help me negotiate the process of becoming at home as a modern human in a woodland environment. I would have liked to be able to consult old-timers and experienced locals, including my dad, but there simply weren't that many around. This is an unfortunate consequence of social change and the realities of aging and death, but I've lately begun to wonder whether my wistfulness amounts to a nostalgia for something that never existed in the first place. The longer I live at the interface where urban boundaries feather and tentacle into undeveloped country, the more I question the applicability of old models of residence.

Living outside the city and beyond cookie-cutter suburbs is in some ways a throwback to an earlier age, but in important ways it's utterly different. Moving to a place because it's pretty or secluded entails a different mindset and different expectations from moving there for the opportunities the land affords for earning a living or providing subsistence. The expertise of the rancher, the farmer, and the timber worker suggests the utility of self-sufficiency, and the failures of some of them illustrate the need for sustainable practices to ensure long-term living in place. But traditional patterns of living don't resolve all the issues and paradoxes that come with trying to live a modern American lifestyle in the wildland interface. The same goes for the ideals of a leave-no-trace wilderness ethic or strict environmentalism: there is much to emulate, but the template is not an exact fit.

I recognize that there are environmental and social implications for living in a relatively undeveloped landscape while also participating in the commercial culture and world of work that characterize the urban environment. Part of my project of becoming at home has been trying to understand some of the obligations, the drawbacks, the demands, and the benefits. I reject the idea that the world exists only to satisfy human desires as well as the opposing extreme, in which human beings are inevitably toxic to the natural environment. The question becomes how best to occupy the boundary zones that are not urban but also not devoid of people. How do we define an ecology of habitation?

Like a wayfarer in a strange country, I was faced with the project of making a home in a new place, of becoming resident in landscape that was integral without my presence. I was uncertain how best to fit in and worried that, despite my earnest and benign intentions, I would commit unintentional offenses. Mostly, though, I tried to stay alert. I looked for the opportunities for discovery and thoughtfulness that my surroundings presented, simply by being their ordinary selves.

· · ·

One morning late in the fall of 1996, Dad woke up and couldn't read the newspaper. He carried on with preparations for that fall's hunting camp and headed into the woods to participate in the autumn ritual that had shaped the annual calendar throughout his life. He shot a nice bull, butchered it, froze the meat, and gave the antlers to Doug that Christmas, saying, "Every vegetarian oughtta have a set of elk horns."

The diagnosis for his headaches and alexia was delivered several weeks later: brain cancer. The first full spring and summer that I lived in the house in Fourmile Canyon thus coincided with a period when I was also reading about neurology, making trips to Denver to lend moral support during radiation treatments, and making and receiving the phone calls that are part of the unhappy routine of terminal illness in our age. I walked to explore our land, but also to escape. Sights and sounds that stirred old memories of camping or fishing trips were rendered more luminous against the backdrop of a slow-moving disaster, as my father's brain was disassembled by the tumor's spreading muck. Watching the links that bound him to his world fray and snap made me sensitive to the cognitive fibers by which we all bind ourselves to the world and to other people.

His death severed the connections between us but initiated for me an extended period of reflection on what he meant to my life, both as an individual and as an example of how to live in this world. I kept wandering and wondering, poking around both outside and in books. Five years after we hung up that first bird feeder, Doug and I left the foothills outside of Boulder to build a new home on a grassy wrinkle in central Colorado, just north of a butte named Cap Rock Ridge. I now work from a different office, with a very different view. I've learned to recognize new birds: western and mountain bluebirds, tree swallows, crossbills, Cooper's and sharp-shinned hawks, gray-crowned rosy-finches, evening grosbeaks, pine siskins, Clark's nutcrackers. I continue to be shaped by the events, some of them large but most of them small, that unfold in the landscape on which I've made my home. I continue to work at tracing the threads between sensation and understanding, between personal experience and the collective wisdom that accrues as people record and share descriptions of the view from their corner of the world.

I'm not a scholar or a researcher, just a homeowner trying to understand what it means to be a resident of these parts. The insights of natural historians and biologists have been helpful, but the scientific tradition that guides such research actively suppresses human sentiment and bias. As someone hoping to create a life in the interface zone that's minimally disruptive to the natural systems that attract me, my observations and experiences are all about emotion and idiosyncrasy. Dispassionate facts have their place in the mosaic that is a place, but substance and nuance come from being *attached*, not detached. Humanity takes a great deal from this world—our food, the materials we use for building and transportation and communication and clothing. Emotionality is one of the ways we give back: with love and respect and gratitude, for sure, but I've also learned to pay attention when I feel anger or frustration or annoyance. These less gratifying emotions usually signal that there's something about my interactions with the environment that I might learn from.

I'm guided by subjectivity, by a pursuit of the singularity of my experience amid the particulars of a location, not by objective ideals or a desire to assemble comprehensive biological case studies. I acknowledge that living where I do exerts pressures on the landscape, but these pages are not a critique of the effects of human development. I work at recognizing and minimizing my impacts where I can, but what follows is not a how-to guide for living lightly. Instead, these are stories, outtakes from my real-life experiences. This book is a travelogue of sorts, a collection of tales from my ongoing journey of being home. We all live someplace. We all occupy an environment, regardless of whether it is characterized by pavement and high-rises or rocks and trees. We're all engaged in a lifelong negotiation with soil and air and people and water and plants and nonhuman animals.

I'm still good at spotting deer and antelope and coyotes and elk, but I've also learned to see the smaller denizens of my environment—flycatchers and blue grama grass and jumping spiders. I still have that first field guide, but it has been joined by a small shelf's worth of fellows: a more detailed guide to western birds, a still more specialized volume dedicated to hawks, and books about plants of the Rocky Mountains, weeds, rare plants of Colorado, mushrooms, animal tracks. A flutter or a pattern or a fleck of color will still capture my attention and impel me to take a closer look. Often, I'll search out the name of the object or phenomenon, and then poke around to discover what other people know about it. Occasionally, the thing that has snagged my eye will lead my mind into a meander, a twisting path along which I think I might find a connection to the larger world. Sometimes, I just pause and look and move on. Now and again, I enter the playground where mind and words caper on a page, documenting a glimpsed event or reliving an experience through a passage of words. I'm still admiring the view out the window, following the drift of my attention with eyes, ears, nose, fingers, and language. When my attention strays, I'm still apt to let my eyes follow the fluttering motions of the birds that pass by.

Voyeur

It's early July, a mild evening after a string of hot days. The sun has dropped below the folds of the foothills behind me. I'm sitting outside on the deck, enjoying the cool air, listening with half an ear to the activity that surrounds the house. The day is still bright but has lost its brassy sheen. A car passes on the road now and again, but most of the noise tonight comes from birds. A nighthawk is swooping over the ridge in front of me, calling out a raspy cry as it circles. It dives every so often, bottoming out with a moaning roar, a sound both eerie and comical. Violet-green swallows wheel and plunge, exchanging quick chirps. Other birds, unseen in the pine branches, have been shrilling for some time now, and I'm trying to block out their incessant noise.

I'm sitting at the metal outdoor table, the house walls ticking behind me as they release the day's store of heat. I'm facing east, away from the road and toward the hillside that rises beyond the pickets of the deck railing. The gravely soil of the slope is stippled with bunch grasses and Oregon grape. Ponderosa pines jut from the hillsides around the house, combing the breeze with their long needles. The air smells faintly of warm dust and pine resin.

I'm writing a letter to a friend, and in a pause between paragraphs I glance up from my writing. A dark brown bird is perched on the cedar birdhouse nailed to a pine tree a dozen yards from the deck.

"Hey!"

I yell at the bird, which is poking its head into the entry of the box. It's obviously trying to get in the birdhouse, and I run down the stairs leading from the deck, with the intention of throwing rocks or pinecones at the interloper. The bird flies away before I can arm myself, and I stomp back up the stairs, muttering. I know that bird doesn't live in the box because I'm familiar with the ones that do. They're small birds, dark gray on top and creamy on the bottom, pygmy nuthatches, according to the slightly washed-out photo in my field guide. I'm no birder, but I've been neighbors with this pair for some time now.

Early in the spring I watched them work at pecking a small round hole into a tall stump on the hillside to the east of our house. Whenever I went outside to get the mail or to water plants, I checked on their progress. At first, I watched the birds as they whittled away at the wood perched on the outside of the stump, but eventually the hole grew deep enough that they were able to work inside, and a light tapping noise was the only outward sign of their project. I would watch and wait for a small gray head to pop out of the neat hole, and if the light was right, I could see the puff of fine wood dust the bird spit out. The head would disappear back inside, and the hollow rapping would resume. This routine transfixed me for weeks, and I often ate my breakfast on the deck, watching and listening to the construction. The muffled taps of the birds' building went on for so long that Doug and I joked that they had decided to add a spare room.

Later in the spring, I was working at my desk, facing west, when I looked up and saw a bear ambling down the hill. Plenty of our neighbors have bear stories, but this was the first time I'd seen one at our house. The animal was young and, as bears go, small and rangy-looking. I snapped a few pictures through the window, but when it climbed a tree and started clawing the bird feeder suspended from it, I ran out on the deck and, for lack of anything better, clapped and shouted like a farmer's wife in a 1950s movie:

"Shoo! G'wan, you, git!"

If I'd been wearing an apron, I no doubt would have flapped it.

The bear stared at me and snuffed deeply a few times. It finally winded me, apparently, because it abruptly jumped down off the tree and ran partway up the hill. It stopped, turned to sniff in my direction briefly, and then shuffled out of sight.

I was excited, but also slightly unnerved. My feelings are often mixed when my life brushes up against the animals that live outside the walls that shelter me. I'm annoyed and yet resigned when I find another plant eaten to green nubs by the deer. I dislike the chipmunks, who also eat my plants; they multiply from the bounty of sunflower seeds the birds spill from the feeder, but I would miss the activity outside my office window if I were to take the feeder down. I'm amused but also feel a faint tingle of guilt when I open the door and discover a small turd left on the doorstep by the resident fox: greeting, warning, territorial mark, or editorial comment? I like it that the windows act as one-way mirrors, obscuring my scent, my movements, and the sounds I make, all the while allowing me to watch the animals beyond the glass. I'm simultaneously privileged and removed.

The evening after the bear's visit, Doug and I began discussing how to hang the bird feeder so the bear couldn't get at it, and whether we should rethink our compost pile.

The next day, I was puttering outside and glanced up to check on the nuthatches. I looked at the stump for several confused minutes before I realized that the tidy round entry had been replaced by a gash. I scrambled up the steep slope for a better look, and sure enough, something had ripped off the front of the wood, exposing the cavity the birds had so patiently pecked out. Grass, hair, and bits of paper trailed in the wind. I was shocked at how deep the pocket was, slung a good six inches below where the entrance had been. No wonder it had taken them so long.

I assumed the bear had destroyed the nest, and I was mad. Then I got even madder, at myself. *This is how it goes, baby*, I silently lectured myself. *The bear was simply doing what bears do. Cycle of life and death, right here for the witnessing. You want nature, you got nature.* Nevertheless, I was furious at the bear for ruining the nest and, I assumed, eating the pygmy nuthatches' eggs. And I was annoyed with myself for the judgment inherent in that attitude. How could I resent the bear for being a predator when I was thrilled one day to glance up from my desk just in time to see the result of a scuffle under the bird feeder: a fox running away with a chipmunk in its mouth?

I did resent the bear, though—detested it, in fact—for undoing the work of the birds I had followed for so long. Among the anonymous flocks that fluttered past the windows, this pair had become familiar, known, and specific. All the weeks of watching them had made me feel like I knew something about their lives.

A few days after the raid on the stump, I noticed a pair of pygmy nuthatches poking around in the birdhouse, which was mounted on a tree not far away. Since no birds had been around the box before the destruction of the nest, I assumed it was the same pair. The box, it seemed, would do in a pinch. I watched them fetch and carry grass and twigs, salvaging some of what remained of the nest in the stump. I cleaned out my hairbrush and snagged the tangle of hair on the bark of a nearby ponderosa pine, a sort of housewarming offering.

Over the next week or so, I watched the birds as they came and went, listened to the tapping that sounded as they arranged newfound nest material. I was relieved to think that the parents had survived and were busy continuing to try to raise their brood, and I smiled whenever I looked at the box and saw a small gray head poking out. More recently, the comings and goings of the parent birds have become all the more obvious, since every time one of them lands at the entry of the birdhouse, a chorus of tiny squeals and chirps erupts from inside. I've been looking forward to seeing the babies emerge, to watching them learn to fly.

• • •

This evening, as I fold my completed letter, I notice that the marauding bird is back, this time perched on the sloping roof of the birdhouse. The parent nuthatches are crying frantically, hopping in quick flights from branch to branch in neighboring trees. I belatedly realize that they have been making the shrill racket I've been trying to ignore all evening, that the predator has been lurking nearby for some time. I fetch the binoculars so I can look at the hunter more closely. The bird matches everything my brain knows about owls, except in miniature. A pygmy owl is hunting the pygmy nuthatches.

The owl flies to a nearby branch and I continue to stare through the binoculars, trying to get them to focus properly. The owl's back is dark brown with light flecks, the belly light-colored and flecked with dark. The bird has a smooth round head and even rounder yellow eyes. Having decided that the owl is too big to fit through the birdhouse entry and get at the baby nuthatches, I can afford to be delighted by the opportunity to observe it. I've never seen a pygmy owl before, and my view of it is close and unobstructed by branches. I stare unashamedly. The owl stares back, blinking. It weaves its head from side to side, examining me suspiciously—perhaps because I've abruptly sprouted my own pair of very round eyes: the outward-facing lenses of the binoculars have a translucent red coating on them, and if owls dream of demons, perhaps they look a little like I do at the moment.

The owl finally gets fed up with my ogling and launches off the branch. It flies obliquely toward the southwest for several wingbeats—and smacks hard into one of the upstairs windows of the house.

I let out a wail, drop the binoculars on the table, and run upstairs. On the planks of the small deck off our bedroom, the owl is sprawled on its back. The wings twitch once or twice, then do not twitch again. I let my knees give way and begin, on the floor, to cry.

I've been wearing a lightweight cotton shirt against the cool of the evening, but I start to overheat, so I take it off and use it to wipe my eyes and blow my nose. I sob as I look at the owl spread-eagled on its back. I'm shaken by the sight of the prone bird, but also by the upwelling of emotion it has provoked. Other birds have brained themselves on our windows over the years, and I was sorry as I carried the feathered parcels away from the house and left them for scavengers. This time, though, I'm not only a witness, I feel responsible: it was my rude stare that triggered this creature's ill-fated flight.

Tears are still seeping from my eyes a few minutes later

when the owl rolls forward and balances itself upright on a tripod formed by fanned wings and tail. I want to bawl harder on seeing the owl alive, but the sound of my distress through the sliding glass door is obviously disturbing the confused bird, so I try to control myself. For a time the owl and I are an awkward tableau: me half-lying, half-sitting on the floor on one side of the doorway, the owl leaning on its wingtips on the other. We're separated only by a screen and a few feet of air, but most of my body is behind the glass of the door, obscured by the kind of reflection that fooled the owl into flying into the window on the adjoining wall. I try to stay still as I watch the bird, attempting to memorize details visible from this close view: the chevron pattern of coffee-colored feathers on the back, the stiffness of the band-ed tail, the round eye sockets, the yellow-gold rings of iris surrounding the pupils' black apertures, the slow-smooth blink, the sleek pivot of the head as the bird looks at me, at the trees beyond the bars of the deck rail, and back at me again. Eventually I move, or sniffle too loudly, and the owl flies off, landing on a branch not far from the box housing the nuthatch nest. The parents resume their frantic chirping and their harassing swoops over the larger bird.

I wipe my nose on my shirt one more time and walk slowly downstairs. With trepidation, I pick up the binocu-lars and look briefly at the owl. It's looking back at me, and I lower the glasses with a burning emotion that feels like shame. The owl ruffles and preens, and a few minutes later it flies away. The nuthatches are finally quiet, and I collapse in a chair. I'm exhausted and pass the rest of the evening in a daze, as if it were my skull and not the owl's that had crashed into a hard illusion. When I go to bed, I'm relieved that both the owl and the nuthatches are alive.

. . .

The next morning, I keep an eye on the birdhouse to see how the pygmy nuthatches have fared, but they're gone. The box is silent. No parent birds fly back and forth with bundles of food in their beaks. I entertain a fantasy that they have spirited the babies away to safety under the cover of darkness. This is lunacy, I know. The babies have been moved from their nest, but not to the safety I would imagine for them.

I move through the day tenderly. The owl is responsible for the silence of the nest. I'm glad the owl is alive. I'm sorry the nuthatches are gone.

Eventually I settle down at my desk and try to work. Outside, nuthatches, pygmy nuthatches, and chickadees make quick sorties at the bird feeder. Juncos, chipmunks, and squirrels sift the sandy soil below, foraging for dropped seeds. Quietly, from my side of the glass, I observe the flit and scurry, the fragments of other lives that pass through the outline of the window's frame. My small gray-and-cream nuthatch parents are out there, perhaps, but if they are I can't tell. My ability to recognize them ended when they fled the box. What had begun to feel like familiarity is gone, and I mourn this, probably, more than the loss of the baby birds, those tiny animals I had never seen.

First Signs

Spring arrives in the high country differently than in other places. Where the land has a strong vertical dimension, the change of seasons is bound to elevation, not distance from the equator. Shades of green swirl up the flanks of mountains as the snow recedes, making the end of winter a complex topographical dance. It's possible to take in the scope of multiple seasons in a single glance: stark black rock laced with winter ice on a mountaintop, looming over new growth shimmering like bottle glass in the valleys below.

I've lived within sight of Colorado's mountains all my life, so my experience with winter's passing is exclusively alpine. I'm conditioned to the idea that spring unfolds cautiously, that it is not a sudden onrush of new foliage and floral outbursts, as I imagine it to be in milder climates. Around here, it takes a while for the planet's slow tipping toward the sun to thaw the ground enough to unleash botanical exuberance, and sudden snowstorms may arrive most any time, setting my heart back to February. Eventually, though, the flake of white drifting in the air is not snow but a small butterfly or moth.

Aside from the dramatic—and welcome—transformation of accumulated snow into water, the first signs of spring in the Rockies are subtle. In high-country meadows, melting snow reveals last year's grasses, ironed hard to the ground. Pressed down for months by the icy residue of blizzards, the fibers are draped across the contours of the land like wet silk. The layers of thatch are lifted from below only with great effort; it takes weeks for pale new growth to nudge its way through and lend a green tint to mountain clearings.

Long before the leaves bud out in willow thickets along streams swollen with runoff, rising sap colors the whiplike stems with startling shades of bright yellow, russet, mahogany, and livid red. I watch the creek beds for the flaring of these finely painted bark geysers and admire the way the sprays merge and diverge in the wind.

The mountain landscape is dominated by evergreens, of course, and it's easy to forget that other trees are up there until new aspen growth stains the slopes with chartreuse patches, bright confetti amid the steadfast and somber shades of pine and spruce.

Spring flowers tend to arrive late and without fanfare. Rather than gaudy swatches of mixed and dancing colors, woodland wildflowers are low-growing, widely spaced, compact, and thrifty. Blooming is a small and intimate affair: lone bouquets of bluebell, heads coyly bowed; tiny bunches of mat daisy recalling scattered flecks of snow; the blossoms of Oregon grape blazing like sunshine beneath spiny scalloped leaves. It takes a more dedicated attention to recognize these displays than it does to admire, say, the lush fur of cherry blossoms, and to sample their fragrance I must seek the flowers' level on hands and knees.

The domination of the vertical in the mountains sometimes makes it difficult to pull away from soaring vistas and the dramatic contrasts of rumpled crags. I'm easily distracted by the swell and jumble of the peaks and miss the small wonders that unfurl between the rocks and evergreens on their slopes. The irony of springtime in the mountains is that its most striking images hug the ground and demand that I unstick my gaze from the overbearing drama of the long-distance view. And while the rewards may seem sparse in comparison to a blaze of azaleas or a hillside carpeted in rhododendrons, the slow rise of spring's tide gives me ample time to look for them. Once it passes me where I live, I only have to follow the snowmelt uphill, and keep my eyes low to the ground.

Lay of the Land

My expectations are still braced for snow, but this early spring day is absurdly warm, and such weather is not to be squandered. I quit my office, grab a jacket, and head outside. Across the paved county road, I walk along the shoulder to the next curve up the hill and, after a hop over the guardrail and a short clamber down the rocks stacked along the road's edge, pick up a trail that meanders through a dense stand of skinny ponderosa pines. Once faint, this path has recently been discovered by mountain bikers, who have worn the pine-needle carpet through to bare soil, smooth and dark. Away from the road, my senses open up and I relax into recognition. The wind exhales through the evergreens in a gently shifting collective sigh that undulates over the hillside. The breeze presses the smell of fresh dirt and a hint of piney resin into my nose.

I pause to pick up the wrapper from a protein bar, which I stuff into the left-hand back pocket of my jeans, the one designated for trash. I tend to leave the older detritus, such as the old tin cans rusting toward filigree or the fragments of antique food crocks I find occasionally. They've been here long enough to begin to reintegrate into the environment: the can housing a spider, the pottery playing host to a colony of lichen. I keep moving past the small skull of a carnivore—most likely a coyote, possibly a dog—that someone recently picked up from the ground and hung, dangling by an eye socket, on a short branch on a pine tree. By virtue of its location, the skull catches my eye the same way candy wrappers and beer cans do; I leave it in place only because it's too high for me to reach.

After a while, the path breaks into a clearing, capped at the far end by a granite outcrop. I clamber up onto one of the rocky knobs and sit. Fourmile Creek chatters below. In summer it's mostly hidden by greenery, but this time of year water glitters between bare gray branches. There hasn't been much snow this winter, and last year's dead vegetation is still standing tall.

The place is "natural," if that's defined as a landscape where human influences are not primary. The trees and shrubs and cacti have chosen their own locations; they grow (or not) according to the conditions of soil and weather, rather than a landscaper's whim. The steeply pitched hillsides, with their deep rocky gullies and granite outcrops, are the result of uplift and erosion rather than engineering. But this is not wilderness by any stretch. From trash to weirdly perched bones to low-flying air traffic passing to and from Denver's airport forty miles away, signs of civilization are easier to find than they are to ignore. The county road that provides access for our house, along with the many dozens of others along this canyon, is a two-lane plateau carved into the hills. I'm sitting within the embrace of one of its many loops; uphill traffic sounds first in my left ear, then behind me, and finally in my right ear, while cars traveling down track from right to left. The chunk of granite on which I'm perched sits under a power line: four heavy gray cables carrying pulses of electric traffic along a route punctuated by weathered and bird-pecked poles.

These are merely the more contemporary, and thereby more obvious, signs that humans occupy the area. You have to look a little closer, get down beneath the tree canopy, to discern the older evidence. Dozens of old mining roads crisscross the slopes around me, terraced onto the hillsides with low stacks of local stone. Sections have collapsed or washed away, and the paths merge, diverge, and fade into one another, but it's still possible to retrace parts of their routes—the newly pioneered bike trail, in fact, knits together a couple of old roads to lead riders downhill to an abandoned railbed in the canyon's bottom. The entire area is pockmarked with mine shafts: some are eerie caves, others mere dips in the land with a barren heap of tailings stacked to the side. There are tangles of antique barbed wire, gun-shot signs, even the twisted carcasses of old cars.

Almost as soon as my eyes register the artifacts of human occupation, my mind enters them into a calculation that assigns a negative value. I'm not sure when this tendency began, and I'm not sure when it became a habit. Less trammeled places offer peace and sustenance, and I'm lucky to live in a place that satisfies these leanings of my sensibilities. But I'm suspicious of monochrome thinking, and this propensity to value the natural over the built threatens to become a lazy routine.

Assigning ideas and objects to paired categories—good/ bad, dark/light, friend/foe—is an ancient adaptation of the human mind. We've long zeroed in on difference and contrast as a way of gleaning information from our surroundings. Cleaving the world-as-influenced-by-people from the world-as-wild certainly offers some useful distinctions, but this scheme discourages attentiveness to continuity and interdependence. Value judgments and an adversarial stance flow all too easily from the resulting binary sets. The place where I now live blurs the lines between the categories of wild and manufactured spaces. Oppositional thinking may well be one of the brain's adaptive conventions, but it's too clumsy an intellectual tool for understanding much that's meaningful about my home territory.

Still, one has to start somewhere. Looking over this steep canyon cut into foothills thickly carpeted with evergreens, I wonder whether the binary habit comes easily here because there is a relative lack of middle ground. What do we call such landscapes, where the human imprint is not integral to the form or use of the land, or where evidence of previous activity appears as a scar? We have words—*bucolic, country, pastoral, idyllic, rural*—that we use in talking about places in which topography and human design have merged so completely as to create a new aesthetic. We describe those areas where the natural has been subsumed as *urban, industrial, built-up, metropolitan. Wilderness* implies a dearth of human interference or transformation. Where engineering and the environment have clashed outright, we use words like *disaster zone, wasteland, eyesore*.

The western settlers who made it over the long haul were those who sought out places with shelter and water—claiming the river bottoms and creek beds and eschewing slopes such as these, where the soil is thin and rocky and the terrain is steep. They survived because they figured out not just how to live on the land, but how to work with it. Some homesteads and ranches in the West fit so well into the landscape that they suggest themselves as an enhancement to their surroundings rather than an affront.

Opportunities for making a long-term living from the land are more scarce up here. Minerals, not agriculture, led settlers into the wrinkles of the Front Range in the late 1800s, and the history of mining in this part of the country is marked by booms and busts more than sustained endeavors. In photos from that time, these foothills look scalped: there are almost no trees, and the scattered cabins look crouched and defensive, squatting on bare expanses of the decomposed granite that passes for soil up here. When the mining economy busted out, towns were abandoned to their ghosts, and the erosive force of gravity began its steady work on the paths and roads and shacks. The scars were eventually carpeted over with evergreens. Nowadays, houses are less exposed than the cabins of old, but their rooflines, driveway cuts, power lines, and window-glint stand out among the trees. Other than the occasional compact log cabin nestled in a natural (or natural-looking) clearing, dwellings here come across, at best, as interruptions in the tree cover and, at worst, as objects that have been tacked onto, imposed upon, or perched on the land.

Homes like the one I live in alter the aesthetic of the landscape, but that aesthetic is what draws residents. Mountain living offers nice scenery and relative tranquility, a sense of serenity and seclusion. People move up here to enjoy the view: wildlife, greenery, and pretty vistas from the windows. Living in such a place provides opportunities for outdoor leisure just outside the front door.

Case in point: I stand up, rub the spots that have gone numb on my fanny, and continue my walk. Being outside, and in the woods particularly, allows me to feel the elemental linkages that bind my corpus to the world. Although I do not make my living from the land, it provokes my sense of what it is to be alive.

Rejoining the trail as it loops downhill, I pause where it fades into a steep eroded slope, the soil bare and loose from skidding bike tires. I leave my own skid marks down the first half, and run the last few steps to a berm of level ground.

Trains once ran alongside this stretch of Fourmile Creek, on a line connecting Boulder to the mining town of Gold Hill. The tracks have long since been removed, but the route leveled for the railroad survives in many areas, including this stretch of canyon. The broad terrace makes a restful interlude on a hike that's otherwise marked by ascent and descent.

Freed from the imperative to watch where I'm putting my feet, I increase my pace and let my gaze wander. A jumble of boulders and cliffs looms over my right shoulder, while to my left, Fourmile Creek engages in a whitewater monologue. I pass a "No Trespassing" sign that was painted onto a rock so long ago that the message is nearly obscured by a creeping rust of pale green lichen. I cross Fourmile Creek with a heel-to-toe creep across a bouncy plank resting on old stone abutments. Here, on the south side of the creek, I'm walking at the base of a steep north-facing pitch, and the ground has not seen sunlight in months. I hustle through the cold air, my shoes thumping on the frosty trail. Eventually I come to a point where another bridge once crossed back over the creek; there is no plank here to span the water, and the runoff from the high country is sufficient to drown all the potential stepping stones under chilly frills of water. I'm not willing to get my feet wet, so I turn around and retrace my steps.

I go a hundred yards or so past the spot where my route joined the railbed, turn left, and begin working my way back uphill along the bottom of a drainage called Sand Gulch. The lower portion requires scrambling over boulders that tumbled down when the county road was blasted into the cliff above. Metal is scattered amid the rocks, which is why, despite the rough going and welcome warmth of the sun, I hustle over the boulders. This is the resting place for the rusting carcasses of five wrecked cars, and I find the spot creepy. The drivers of these vehicles presumably took the corner up above too fast, although it's possible some of the cars were stolen and pushed over the brink for the thrill of the mess and the crash. Judging from the vintages, the accidents happened thirty or forty years ago, but an air of violence still lingers around the mangled passenger compartments and far-flung panels.

The continued presence of the old wrecks would seem to contradict my theory that people move up here for the scenery: surely if this were so, someone would have hauled the hulks out long ago. The sides of the canyon are steeply pitched, however; the only land with a view onto this area is on the far side of Fourmile Creek, publicly owned and roadless.

The perspective that land can earn its keep simply by being pretty would seem to be a step forward for human enlightenment, but on this point, too, I am ambivalent. My issue isn't with aesthetic valuation in itself, but rather with the difficulties of managing self-interest in the calculus of such judgments, since personal aesthetics don't always jibe with local conditions. Plenty of properties show the lengths to which landowners will go to make their acreage look as if it belongs somewhere else—usually a location with much higher annual precipitation. Other people seek out woodland settings for the recreational opportunities they provide. Some of them consider land that can't be accessed for hiking, mountain biking, allowing dogs to run, or riding ATVs to be either underutilized or worthless.

A more subtle quandary plays out in the context of that nature-equals-good and built-equals-bad dichotomy. In those old photos, the landscape that looked scalped to me probably aligns more closely with the "natural" state of these hills than today's carpeting monocrop of ponderosa pines. Most of the mature trees had been cut when the images were made, rendering the land more bald than it should have been, but healthy ponderosa forests are characterized by grassy expanses as much as tree cover. The forest around me today is composed of spindly trees growing too close to one another to mature properly, their trunks crooked and leaning in a quest for light. The soil beneath these dog-hair stands, cast in perpetual shade by a thatch of boughs and incessantly showered with pine needles, is acidic and starved of the humus that accumulates when grasses and forbs grow, die, and decompose in a normal cycle. The trees sprout and grow of their own volition and without the management of people, but the overly dense forest is very much a product of human effort, in the form of our century-old institution of fire suppression. The forest is sickly and a conflagration waiting to happen, but many residents seem loathe to take on the project of thinning. I'm not sure whether this inaction springs from ignorance or indifference, but I suspect that some assume that whatever the landowner did not plant is "natural" and thereby superior.

I wish there were a do-it-yourself manual that would allow me, in one easy weekend, to make it look as if my house had grown right out of the ground. I wish that I could know what not to plant and how to successfully nurture the flora best suited to this place. I wish I were better at not harassing or cultivating bad habits in wildlife, wish I had the time and resources and know-how to restore a sizable expanse of conifer forest. The desire for quick fixes is, however, barely one step removed from the simplistic monochrome of black and white thinking I'm trying to avoid. The amicable merging of human and wild domains that I would like to conjure cannot arise quickly. There isn't a fixed protocol that will bring it about in a week or a month or a year. The county commissioners cannot write the bucolic into the land-use code.

Again, one has to start somewhere, and I have to believe that paying attention is a worthy first step. Balmy weather aside, the project of being attentive is the prod that sends me out of the house periodically on walks such as this. I walk and watch and listen, gleaning details and seeking patterns. I want to emulate the character of those beings and landforms that have coexisted here over the long term. I'm hoping I'll be able to adapt my rhythms, to find ways to naturalize according to the realities—not the ideals—of my surroundings. I aspire to balance the desires provoked by my society with my station as an animal living in a particular environment.

At the edge of the boulder field, I fight my way through a thicket of willows interwoven with the canes of wild roses hairy with thorns. On the far side of the shrubby tangle, I join a game trail that runs alongside a trickle of water. The seasonal flow, which disappears underground at the boulder field, gurgles through channels cut in stone and flows silently between humped banks of soil. The stream is small, fewer than a dozen inches wide in most places, but it nurtures narrow-leafed cottonwoods, alder, more wild roses, and thick grass. I enter another pocket of cold air at the base of a low cliff, where mats of moss grows in the perpetual shade. In summer I'm inclined to pet the mats as if they were cats, but today the moss is dormant and stiff and I keep walking. For a couple of hundred yards, the path along the drainage—deep enough in the gulch to muffle the sound of cars on the road, groomed by the passage of deer and coyotes rather than mountain bikes, a diverse woodland rather than an evergreen monocrop—offers the ambiance of a naturalistic ideal: complex, intertwined, quietly efficient.

Eventually, the drainage splits; one branch, dry except when carrying water from summer thunderstorms, heads uphill to my right, while Sand Gulch carries on straight ahead. A grassy triangular glen flanked by cottonwoods spreads out between the two drainages. In summer, the trees' leaves provide a steady background noise of arrhythmic rattles and slaps, but today the bare branches are silent.

Scattered in the grass near the right side of the glen is what's left of the skeleton of a deer: some leg bones, a curve of vertebrae linked in a column, the frame of a pelvis. On this same walk two years ago, I nearly tripped over the carcass which was, on that day, still fresh enough that only the soft tissues of the body cavity had been eaten. A compacted lump of chewed grass that had been in the stomach lay nearby; although peeled of its viscera, the lump retained the distinctive shape—a combination of curves and rounded planes—of an internal organ.

I could not help but imagine that the buck, suffering fatal injuries from being hit by a car, made his way down to this quiet vee of grass to die. It's rare to be able to single out a particular individual from the deer population with which we share the neighborhood, other than sorting the males from the females, the young from the adults. By the distinctive asymmetrical branching of the antlers, however, I recognized the dead buck as one of the culprits that would blithely browse on the plantings that serve as our yard until I ran out onto the deck and hollered. Although I'd felt regret when I first found him, I'd been unable to suppress the thought that this deer, at least, wouldn't be eating my succulents any more.

I decided that the dead buck offered me an opportunity to observe decomposition, one of the more frank natural processes that I, in the company of many of my fellow modern citizens, tend to shield myself from. I made a point of visiting the body now and again over the next several months to mark the stages of the deer's disintegration back into the wider environment. Muscle and hide were eaten away over a period of weeks, outlasted by the lump of partially digested grass, which took months to dissolve. I was able to maintain my amateur naturalist's cool as ribs were nibbled shorter and shorter and the leg bones scattered, until the day that the carcass, nearly down to its bare bones, was crawling with ants and beetles. This, apparently, marked the limit of my tolerance for raw nature: I hurried away all a-shudder and did not return until I felt certain the bones would be picked clean. All that remains now are abstract white forms, cracked and brittle, going slowly to ground.

Today I'm thinking less about death and decay than about my psyche's habit of preferring the natural over the built. Is this why I watched the deer break down yet have avoided making any similar observations of the wrecked cars? The carcasses, bone and metal alike, are undergoing decomposition and decay, each according to the timeline dictated by their elements. Is the moldering of the cars simply too slow—too slow for my eyes to discern, too slow for the dissolution to make appreciable progress in the span of time I've lived here? Is it that the cars, with their busted-out windows and far-flung doors, too vividly suggest human death, violent and bloody? Is it easier to contemplate mortality in the decomposition of an animal, a being with lifeways and a culture so different from my own? And is this about mortality at all? Maybe it's about trashiness. I picked up the food wrapper because it's out of place. The old cans with their resident spiders and pieces of crockery with their blotches of lichen have been here long enough to begin to go native. But if I could justify the expense, I'd have the old cars hauled off the boulder pile—although surely they've become homes for more than the odd spider.

In the end, I keep coming back to this: the deer's bones belong. The cars don't. It boils down to aesthetics. Picking up the fresh trash, or even taking the canine skull out of the tree and putting it back down on the ground where it "belongs," is a matter of taste.

And precisely because it is a matter of taste, I feel the need for caution. Aesthetic judgments are reflective: they mirror the observer, not the object of scrutiny. Their slick rational-izations lead me back to where I started, basing my rela-tionship to the land on what pleases me. Declaring that the woods should remain untouched (once the house is built) or landscaping with delusions of precipitation or pursuing unrestricted outdoor recreation: any of these scenarios makes me feel like even more of a burden on this pretty but beaten-up land.

The effort to push beyond the personal, to see myself and my life in the context of this place, leads me back to the idea of the bucolic. The harmonious landscapes evoked by the concept suggest that the choices made in them transcend mere personal preference. Prettiness may play a part, but what matters in the long term is what works in the environ-ment and what doesn't, what's sustainable in a given loca-tion and what's not. Trying to emulate a coastal woodland in a semiarid midcontinent setting is certainly an aesthetic choice, but it will never achieve pastoral harmony. The envi-ronment can't support it; without the gardener's heroic in-terventions, the verdant vision can only wither and die. If local conditions aren't factored in, the environment becomes a foe to be battled against. This is the mentality of a boom economy: forcing the landscape to yield its resources with-out regard to long-term viability. When booms go bust, the people move on. The land remains, but it is frequently eco-logically impaired, sometimes toxic, and often ugly.

In their ideal form, bucolic landscapes succeed, survive, and appeal because they result from choices that are com-patible with local conditions rather than from an insistence on what's pretty or what maximizes immediate profit. Their harmonious character arises out of a collaborative synergy between human efforts and natural processes. People have altered the landscape, but within the framework of the native vernacular. Such places demonstrate that the human animal is capable, even in the modern era, of coexisting with the natural world, that we are capable of altering the landscape without destroying its integrity.

I leave the quiet glen via yet another game trail, scrambling up toward the road and arriving at the pavement out of breath. After a few hundred yards of walking along the shoulder, I cross, check the mailbox—too early—and head up toward the house. There's still a rawness to our place, and I don't know whether the house will ever achieve the kind of grown-in-place appearance and easy companionability with the evergreens and rocky gulch that I envision and hope for. Still, there are signs of progress, and they keep me going. The dog-hair stand of ponderosa pine just east of the house, which we thinned a few years ago, is becoming more of a dappled space. The ground beneath the remaining trees, opened up to sunlight and relieved of some of its annual burden of acidic pine needles, sprouts a little more grass each year.

The front steps are surrounded by terraced planters built, in the manner of the old roads, from stacks of native stone. Cultivating the beds is an ongoing experiment, an annual rite of replacing plants that succumb to weather, aridity, or browsing wildlife. The results are in no danger of being mistaken for a formal garden, and I suspect that even a cottage gardener would snicker, but the plantings are maturing to a low-water, low-maintenance state. When they're in full flush in midsummer, the beds are sufficiently verdant to qualify as a garden yet compact enough to not seem ostentatious in the dry climate. They stand out from the woodland background, but do not seem out of place.

Nestled among the scrappy plants and the stacked stones is the stark white skull of a deer, complete with a set of distinctively asymmetrical antlers. After the bugs had done their work down in the secluded glen, I lugged the skull home. It was an aesthetic choice, a touch of western iconography for the front of the house. Quite aside from its Georgia O'Keeffe flair, the skull is frankly beautiful: the nasal passages are twinned vortices of spongy mesh coiled beneath the sleek planes of the cheekbones; suture joints knit the plates of the skull together across the forehead with intricate loops like the gooseneck flow of meandering rivers. The shapely tines of the antlers rise and branch among the winter-dried stems and leaves, as if they belong there.

Where Does Your Garden Grow?

On a small deck opening off our top-floor bedroom, I have a garden. It's not elaborate, but a variety of vegetables, herbs, and a few flowers grow serenely in a hodgepodge of containers: plastic, square, terra cotta, round, rectangular. Nasturtiums dangle from a hanging basket lined with coconut husk; purple basil grows in a tall can that once held olive oil; and white daisies stand up straight in a small strawberry pot, sporting a skirt of blue-flowered lobelia. From below, tomatillos and peppers wave cheerily between the vertical posts of the railing, and a cucumber vine trails along the gutter. Behind them grow a few tomato plants, Swiss chard, different varieties of basil, beets, eggplant, and a dwarf apple tree with a hummingbird feeder suspended from one branch.

The harvest isn't huge—mixed salad occasionally, some herbs for cooking. I won't know for a few more weeks whether there will be eggplant for a stir-fry or fixings for a batch of homegrown, homemade salsa. We enjoy the greenery, however, not just on our plates, but also before our eyes and rustling softly on the wind outside the open bedroom door on summer nights. I'm partial also to the smell of damp earth drifting cleanly in the air after I water. And I like to stroll the deck planks—about five paces is all it takes—and admire the variety of color, form, and texture assembled in that small area.

What's odd about all this is that I'm growing a city garden in the country. The veggies on our bedroom deck aren't leaning over streets filled with honking cars or quick-walking pedestrians. The world I watch going by when I lean on the rail is populated by ponderosa pines, lichen-crusted boulders, mule deer, bunchgrass, chipmunks, sage, and, occasionally, an ash-gray fox that has a den somewhere nearby.

Although there are precious few flat spots to till a garden in this steep terrain, the issue isn't a shortage of space so much as the neighbors. Planting a garden here is like opening a gourmet salad bar for the local wildlife. The chipmunks, rabbits, and deer have been quick to expand their tastes to imported herbs, exotic flowers, and fancy greens. Well-watered and succulent, I'm sure these plants are a welcome change from the tough and wiry native flora.

But since I'm not willing to share my crop, I started growing most of my vegetable plants in containers on the large deck fronting the main floor of our house a few years ago. This kept the deer out, but the chipmunks and rabbits quickly mastered the stairs and helped themselves to haute cuisine. The rodents didn't just steal strawberries, tomatoes, tomatillos, and lettuce leaves, but lopped down entire eggplant plants, chopped branches off geraniums, pulled up pansies by the roots, and beheaded marigolds. Every morning I would walk out the front door to find limp new victims.

Though we could put up a tall permanent fence all around the house, I would feel like we were living in a compound, so late last summer I became a city-style gardener in a woodland setting. One by one, I carried the pots and their nibbled contents into the house, up the stairs, through the bedroom, and out onto the upstairs deck, which has no access from outside. This last spring I lugged more pots, more dirt, and more mulch through the house, then wired a hose to the wall outside so I didn't have to carry water from the bathtub.

Nowadays, when I need some herbs or want to fix a salad, I head up to the bedroom instead of out the kitchen door. So far this year I've picked two cucumbers, lots of lettuce and beet greens, a few hot peppers, and several pear-shaped yellow tomatoes. I'm ready to harvest basil for my second batch of pesto. My hope is that, sometime later this summer, I'll walk out of the bedroom one afternoon cradling a glossy purple eggplant or two. I'm fond of gently squeezing the papery husks of the tomatillos to feel the little green fruits swelling inside. As long as the chipmunks and rabbits don't take up climbing, things are looking good for that salsa.

Five Ways of Seeing a Mountain Lion

We are eating dinner outside at the end of a hot summer day: avoiding the stuffy house, sipping wine, waiting for the air to begin moving again. Hummingbirds bicker at the feeder.

An outburst of crashing brush and animal cries in the gulch west of the house ends before we can jump out of our chairs, but we run to the other side of the deck anyway, peering toward the rocky notch. No animals, no movement. The quiet following the ruckus is inlaid with the faint trickle of water threading over rocks and the feet of slim cottonwoods in the bottom of the gulch. The snapping tree branches had suggested a large animal. Neighbors have reported seeing a bear recently. We elect not to investigate more closely.

Later, from the living room, I hear the mewling bleat of a fawn. Once again I dash to the deck rail. This time I see a young deer, no longer spotted but born this past spring. And another animal. Motionless in a break between pines, it is watching the deer run away. My eyes and brain try to decide what it is, but I am not certain until I see the end of a long J-curve of tail twitch.

Mountain lion. Large. I have just enough time to register this information before the cat walks silently out of sight.

II.

The mountain lion I saw had a coat the hue of well-cooked toffee: not tawny. The species' scientific name, *Puma concolor*, means cat of one color. Cat of one color, but many names: mountain lion or mountain cat, catamount, panther, puma, cougar. The etymology of these names—multiple English forms, *puma* from the Quechua language family of the Andes via French, *cougar* from the Tupi of Brazil via Portuguese and French—points to a history of encounters with native peoples and Europeans along an elongated frontier. Mountain lion habitat extends from northern Canada to the southern Andes. This range was once even larger, stretching from coast to coast in what is now the United States. Only humans range more widely along the length of the Western Hemisphere.

Mountain lions are crepuscular, meaning they are most active at dawn and dusk. They are solitary animals, except for a few days while mating and when a female is raising her young. Females raise the kittens on their own, and young mountain lions stay with their mother for up to two years. Males occupy territories of one hundred to two hundred square miles, which can encompass the territory of several females. Males are intolerant of other males, but female territories may overlap, and daughters often establish territories near those of their mother.

Population estimates for mountain lions in Colorado range from three thousand to seven thousand. This high degree of uncertainty intimates the cats' reclusiveness and wide-ranging habits.

III.

Mountain lions prefer territory with a mix of trees, shrubs, and rock outcrops. Unlike open land, such terrain facilitates their ambush style of hunting. Mountain lions stalk their prey, attack, and apply a killing bite to the back of the neck. The position of injuries, to the base of the skull rather than the throat, helps identify mountain lion predation, as does the size of the wounds inflicted by the teeth.

As obligate carnivores, mountain lions must eat meat to survive. In most of their range in North America, deer are their preferred prey, although they will also eat smaller mammals such as raccoons. Prey recognition is learned behavior, passed from mother to offspring. Humans are not generally recognized as prey, although attacks on people do occur. I saw the mountain lion from a distance, from a second-floor deck. These factors did not stop my heart from thumping in somatic recognition that technology and book-learning have not removed me from the food chain.

IV.

Bears and wolves compete with mountain lions for food but do not habitually hunt them. Humans are the only species that regularly preys on mountain lions. European settlers extirpated them from the eastern portion of their range in the continental United States before the United States became a nation.

Five years after it became a state in 1876, Colorado began offering a bounty on mountain lions. In 1965, they were reclassified as a big game species and are currently managed as such. The Colorado Division of Wildlife instituted an annual harvest limit system in 1975, in which quotas are set for game management territories across the state. Hunters are required to call a hotline before starting a hunt, to ensure that harvest limits for the area they plan to hunt in have not been met. If they have, the area is closed to further hunting for the remainder of the season.

Harvest quotas are broken down by gender to help prevent overhunting of females. Individuals applying for a license to hunt a mountain lion in Colorado are required to pass a written test that includes details on how to determine the sex of the animal before it is killed. Mountain lions are hunted with packs of up to eight dogs. The dogs tree the lion, which is then shot at close range.

V.

When I told my brother Dennis about the encounter over the phone, he said, "I've never seen a mountain lion." His voice was wistful. He began hunting deer and elk at an early age and has spent more time in the backcountry than I am ever likely to.

That I have seen a mountain lion and he has not is ironic, but not surprising. The area around Boulder and Denver has a higher prey density than some undeveloped parts of the state. Irrigated and fertilized lawns and gardens attract deer, as does illegal feeding. Along with the lush ornamental landscaping, accessible pet food, garbage, and water also attract the raccoons, skunks, and other small mammals that serve as prey for mountain lions. Cats and dogs are small mammals. Like human beings, mountain lions are widely distributed because they are adaptable. The presence of people, homes, and roads is not a strong enough deterrent to overcome the attraction of plentiful prey occupying a landscape that offers ample cover for ambush hunting.

From the remembered vibration of its pounding, I know my heart does not comprehend the assessment that mountain lions do not favor humans. But the presence of an ambush hunter is not a strong enough deterrent to overcome the attraction of taking solitary walks in this landscape, with its mix of trees, shrubs, and rock outcrops.

I am more cautious now. Even in bright midday sunshine, I scan the ground for tracks, check slopes and rock ledges above my head for yellow eyes. I watch for a brush of brown hide, a twitching tuft of tail between conifer boughs. I struggle to identify the sounds coming from unseen sources in the folded landscape. I have stopped walking alone at dusk.

Attentiveness may be merely prudent, but it is intended also as a gesture of deference. I have seen a mountain lion once. I am certain that mountain lions have seen me many times. The lion is a reminder that I live not merely at an address, but in an ecosystem. My presence here affects the mountain lion. The mountain lion affects me.

Love Letter to a Sewage Lagoon

Folded mountains are the topography of home. To my eyes, the horizon is properly serrated by peaks, and the dominant background color is the black-green hue of conifer trees. The scents of pine and spruce, sharp as their needles, are comforting, as is the soft rustle of wind through their branches. Shadowed creek beds, wildflowers crouched in the understory, the chatter of birds hidden in crisscrossing branches: such details are so familiar that I sometimes have to remind myself to notice them.

During childhood camping trips, I slept under tarps in the San Juan Mountains of southwestern Colorado, near lakes or rivers where Dad led the family on his time off. In the mid-1970s, when my parents were able to afford a boat, we began to also camp on the rocky shores of Navajo Lake, a nearby reservoir. We ate catfish and crappie rather than trout, the ground was sun-blasted and rocky rather than shaded and padded with duff, and the sky when I stretched out in my sleeping bag was a broad expanse of stars unfringed by pine boughs. Even so, the landscape was pretty familiar, since Navajo was barely an hour's drive south of where we lived.

Lake Powell was another matter entirely. Powell was a half-day drive and another world away. I remember jouncing over the dirt roads that accessed Hall's Crossing on those first trips into Utah, the bow of the boat jiggling in the dust out the rear window of the camper shell. My brothers and I rode in the back of the pickup, reclining on sleeping bags and camping mattresses amid the rattle of chuck boxes, ice chests, cases of beer, fishing gear, and cans of pop. Through the side windows, the view shifted from forested mountainsides to sandy flats flecked with piñon and cut by dry washes, then finally to a landscape dominated by sandstone. A sea of rock spread around us, rising and falling in rounded waves. Cliffs rose up like islands, or the sides of huge ships.

We watched hoodoos, mushrooms, domes, cones, cracks, buttes, and notches roll past the windows, all composed of bare sandstone, pink and tan. The black streaks of desert varnish staining sheer rock faces were a visual echo of the streamers of virga trailing from distant thunderheads. Amphitheaters arched across rock faces like eyebrows. Green tufts of cottonwood gleamed incongruously in canyon bottoms. Holes opened on cliff faces, sometimes grouped in rows like choruses of singing mouths.

We arrived at the boat ramp at Hall's Crossing, where a flat expanse of blue-green lake stretched before us: the age-old miracle of water in the desert writ large. When the boat sliced beyond the broad bay on which the marina was situated, we entered a canyon where walls of solid rock rose straight up from the water's surface. There were no trees, no distant vistas, nothing but planes of liquid and stone intersecting at sharp angles. As we rounded each curve in the watercourse, the walls closed behind us and a new segment of the canyon opened: the long narrow lake revealed itself like a scroll. Aside from the twin white lines of distant vapor trails and the occasional passing boat, it seemed that the vessel I was riding in was the only manufactured thing in a world otherwise composed simply of water, sky, and rock.

In the impressionable brain of my preadolescent years, the contours of this landscape pressed in deep. In the mountains, with their fur of evergreens, I had always felt soothed and at home. But the desert's undisguised geography was a new kind of terrain, a place where the land was not hidden by a pelt of grass and trees and was flayed, even, of all but occasional patches of soil skin. In its strangeness, the desert called attention to fundamental details about my surroundings: the smell of water, the blare of sun against my skin. The whispers and chatters of foliage were absent. Hiking across slickrock, I left no tracks. In the canyons or from the bottom of a split of stone, the sky was a ribbon instead of a dome. Climbing out of those rock notches sent the horizon into a dizzying retreat, as the press of rock around me was abruptly replaced by vastness.

I don't think there's a set formula for falling in love, but surprise, wonder, the invitation to thoughtfulness, and meeting the other on its own terms all have a role in the process. I inherited much of my devotion to the mountains from my father, but Lake Powell provided me with the opportunity to discover the character of one small part of the world for myself. On the shores of that paradoxical desert lake, I learned what it meant to fall in love with a place.

Love, of course, is seldom simple, and it wasn't long before complications set in. Lake Powell had the power and presence of wildness—beauty, mercurial weather, indifference to the well-being of the human individual—but a representative of untrammeled nature it was not. Although it often seemed as if boats were the only sign of human technology, I knew that the lake itself was a reservoir, a gigantic human artifact imposed on the red rock land.

My oldest brother, Dale, a fan of Edward Abbey and an aspiring monkey-wrencher, talked about Glen Canyon, a narrow, deep, and wondrous river gorge now drowned under the waters of Lake Powell. I walked into enough side canyons, sipped from enough potholes, admired enough hanging gardens, stared up the sheer face of enough cliffs, rested in enough puddles of cottonwood shade, and poked my head into enough Indian ruins to have an inkling of what was lost when the reservoir filled. Later I would find out that the Colorado River no longer flows into the ocean, would learn how the Glen Canyon Dam helped foul the dynamics of an entire river system.

Reading Abbey's books myself, I discovered that he put words to some of my feelings for the desert. These writings resonated deeply for me, even though my sole experience of the slickrock desert transpired, for years, along the shoreline of a reservoir that Abbey despised. He called Lake Powell—the waters of which I saw as an oasis, which I drank, played in, slept beside, and ate fish from—a "sewage lagoon."

. . .

A few years ago, I was standing in the living room at a neighbor's house and saw a perfectly round sphere of ruddy sandstone displayed on a ledge. I picked it up and rolled it in my hand, recognition stirring in the heft and grittiness of the orb. I said that we used to find them at Lake Powell and asked, "Is that where this one came from?"

Our neighbor, a dedicated environmental activist, said crisply, "We hate Lake Powell."

I set the stone ball back down and became shy about professing an affection for Lake Powell beyond the circle of people who shared my history there. As I've become more tuned in to issues of conservation and environment, the divergence between the tenderness of my memories and the environmental dimensions of Lake Powell has become wider, and my affections more complicated still. To many people, the reservoir is a potent symbol of overweening human ambition, of unsustainable appetites for electricity and water, of a disregard for the subtleties of natural systems. I acknowledge the arrogance, the folly, the ignorance, and I recognize the weight of these legacies across the western lands that I know and love. When I read about the movement to remove the dam, part of me sympathizes, but part of me mourns. I grieve at the thought of losing the place that holds some of the most clearly defined memories of my childhood.

A bridge is usually a plane of access across water, but for me the waters that drowned Glen Canyon were themselves a bridge, a gangway toward the desert's interior. I might have never ventured to that stark and thirsty country—at least not while I was young enough to develop such an unconditional affection—if it weren't for the reservoir's waters, floating our pale blue boat across the lost fissure of Glen Canyon.

When I seek out slickrock nowadays, I go to places that are more true to their arid character. I don't climb into a boat but strike out on foot, into the red rock country that has become the place I crave when I wish to be reminded in blunt, tangible terms that I am defined by what lies beyond my skin, when I feel the need to remember what is elemental in myself. The nakedness of the desert invites feelings of intimacy, yet the harshness and strangeness of the land make me feel vulnerable. Yes, it is still very much like love.

Someone like my neighbor might assert that moving through a landscape less modified than the shoreline of a reservoir, under my own power, constitutes a more mature love of place than my childhood crush on the engineered shores of Lake Powell. I would agree that my relationship to the desert has grown up, but I also recognize that any elevation of my sensibilities toward that environment—or any other aspect of the natural world—has been built on experiences with developed and altered landscapes. Establishing a relationship with a place—extending my heart toward an entity that did not return my devotion with gifts or hugs or words—was more vital to the development of an environmental ethic than the degree of natural purity exhibited by the object of my affection.

I'm haunted by thoughts of what was lost beneath the waters of Lake Powell, but I have not learned to hate that place. I've decided that I can't afford to dismiss this opportunity to feel tenderness, despite the murk from which it springs.

Reaping an Unexpected Harvest

At best, I'm still a novice when it comes to gardening. I'm plagued by grandiose visions of lush plantings brought on by the seductive pictures in gardening magazines and seed catalogs. I tend to engage in fantasies of organic produce and eye-pleasing flowers more often than I apply myself to the chores of watering and weeding.

I keep at it though, and not simply because I covet home-grown veggies and bouquets. I know I'll never be the kind of serene and generous soul who is satisfied simply with watching things grow, but patience and attentiveness, qualities I associate with gardening, are attributes I'd like to cultivate in myself.

If progress in this self-improvement project is slow, it does come. And one of the things I'm learning is that the lessons may arrive from oblique angles. Take composting, for example. On the surface, fermenting yard waste to use for fertilizer seems pretty straightforward, but on the spring afternoon when I first opened up the panels at the bottom of the compost bin, I caught a glimpse of something bigger.

Compared with stabbing a shovel into a bag from the local discount store, the experience of scooping do-it-yourself fertilizer out of the composter verged on the sublime. The conversion of slimy kitchen scraps and botanical refuse into this dark and crumbly material was wondrous to my eyes and nose. Shoveling the homemade compost into five-gallon buckets was like harvesting hope.

Setting that solemn event aside for a moment, it seems likely that I find composting gratifying because it requires comparatively little work. Hauling cuttings and kitchen slop out to the composter is hardly my favorite chore, but my husband takes his turn at it too, so it's really not so bad. And while turning the pile doesn't happen as regularly as it should, I get serviceable results. Composting is also satisfying because it redeems many of my failures. Withered plants for whom the water came too late still have a place in the garden, along with those that have been fatally nibbled by deer or chipmunks and those that are blackened by frosts I should have anticipated. These victims of my procrastination and inattention go into the compost bin, along with eggshells, banana peels, squash rinds, onion skins, and fronds trimmed off the houseplants.

The path out to the composter has become a link that joins my pampered and modernized indoor lifestyle to deep and ancient rhythms. I enjoy participating in the age-old cycle by which new life feeds off the remains of the old, without my own carcass being involved. I admire the economy of it all, the recycling of detritus into something fragrant and useful.

Like so many things in life, however, composting is fraught with the unexpected.

Whether from insufficient time, too little moisture, or a lack of heat, my first batch of compost was undercooked, a little raw. Effective as fertilizer—this year's plants are larger, more robust and productive than last year's—the compost has also been the carrier of an array of volunteer seeds. What I had hoped were hollyhocks sprouting where I had, in fact, planted hollyhock seeds, turned out instead to be squash. Having gotten a late start, the plants are tiny in midsummer and have little chance of maturing before the snow flies, but they're resolute, steadily putting out small yellow blossoms shaped like stars. I noticed a miniature acorn squash resting between the sage and lemon thyme the other day; I doubt it will be edible, but it's pretty, and the vine on which it's growing fills in some of the bed's bare patches.

Another group of plants, which I've finally identified as tomatillos, are making a go of it among the powdery green spears of the iris. Once again, they're dinky and no doubt doomed, but I haven't the heart to pull them out. It's hard to get anything to grow in the poor soil and dry conditions here. Discouraging these little squatters makes me feel like a thug.

And I must confess to a peculiar fondness for the upstarts from the compost bin. Unlike the wiry natives, Mediterranean-adapted herbs, and various weeds that populate the planting beds around the house, the squash plants and tomatillos have survived a trial by fire. They've evaded the forces of decomposition and, in defiance of their long-term odds, they're growing. Even though I know they're soaking up water that could be going to the plants I've taken the trouble to select, position, and set in the ground, I'm swayed by their tenacity. Their incongruity is both endearing and reassuring.

There's no question I'm pleased when I harvest a bowl of lettuce or keep the rosemary alive over the winter. But seeing errant green sprigs rising after I've dosed a patch of ground with my homemade compost evokes an odd satisfaction as well. The pleasure is different from that of finding a seed variety that grows well under local conditions or mastering the basics of pest management. The tomatillos among the iris and the squash winding through the herbs offer a lesson about the vigor and assertiveness of living things that's harder to discern in well-plotted plantings. Unplanned and unexpected, the volunteers from the compost help me understand that being a gardener isn't about being in control. They counsel me to remember that diligence is balanced by standing back, and so they tutor me toward those intangible and inedible goals having to do with patience and paying attention.

Growing contentedly in their unconventional places, these tender shoots remind me that observation, too, is a kind of harvest. I sit down on a stone bench for a few minutes to contemplate all the plants that make up my garden. Regardless of their points of origin, they are putting down roots and unfurling new leaves, each seeking its own angle toward the light.

A Walk in the Park

The tallest sand dunes in North America rise at neither the Atlantic nor the Pacific coast. They're landlocked, in fact, nestled against the western flank of the Sangre de Cristo Mountains in south-central Colorado. The dunes are made up of grit picked up by the prevailing winds blowing across the elongated pan of the San Luis Valley. As the wind meets the toothed blade of the Sangres, it sweeps upward and drops its accumulated load of sand, forming dunes that crest to more than seven hundred feet above the valley floor.

The Great Sand Dunes National Park and Preserve is near Highway 160, the main east-west route across southern Colorado. The park also isn't far from Highway 285, which runs north and south. Throughout my childhood and youth, whether going to visit my grandparents, to stay with Mom after she and Dad split, or commuting between Boulder and Durango during college vacations, I endured countless road trips through the valley and past the dunes.

Always *past* the dunes. The brown and white signs pointing toward the monument (the area's expansion to park status was finalized in 2004) were well-known landmarks. Like the pale smudge of the dunes themselves as seen from a distance, the signs were part of the roadside scenery that cut deep memory traces in my brain over the years. Whether I was a passenger or driver, the familial habit was to travel the monotonous arrow-straight stretches of road through the San Luis Valley without stopping and with the speedometer nudged somewhere over the speed limit.

One day, at the age of twenty-three, I was driving between Boulder and Durango and decided to stop at the dunes. Instead of blowing past the sign at sixty-five or seventy miles per hour, I slowed and turned. As I approached, the familiar buff-colored patch of ground at the foot of the Sangres grew into hills, then into a towering landscape of sweeping curves and rounded summits. The flowing patterns contrasted sharply with the sage scrub of the nearby valley and the jagged blue pinnacles of the mountains. I paid my fee, parked, and, crossing the small stream at the hem of the dunes, felt as if I had been transported out of the Rockies and into the Sahara. A plain of sand stretched before me, then began to rise. I hiked up into the private folds of the dunes between peaks of sand and spent a few hours up there. The parking lot, other people, trees, and even, at times, the neighboring mountains vanished. I scrambled up and down slopes and traversed crests. Huffing from walking in loose footing at high altitude, I would lie down and stare up at the sky, warm sand against my back like a fancy massage. Rolling over, I examined the stitchlike patterns left by the feet of beetles and mice and pushed handfuls of sand over the crests of dunes, watching the grains pour downward like a silken drape, the shifting arrangement of texture and dampness offering the illusion of shimmer. The air was clean, with subtle scents of mineral and salt, and except when a breeze stirred their surface to a whisper, the heavy dunes absorbed sound and provided a near-perfect embrace of solitude and stillness. I was sorry to leave but eventually started plodding toward the parking lot, striding down steep slopes with giant steps. In the car later on, the grit of the dunes still between my toes, I felt more than a little sheepish about all the times I had bypassed that remarkable place.

. . .

National parks were not part of my experience growing up. I'm not certain what my father thought of them, but the evidence of my childhood suggests his opinion wasn't high. Other than the odd day trip to the nearby Anasazi ruins at Mesa Verde, Chaco Canyon, or Hovenweep, family vacation time involved camping, and camping meant, as much as possible, escaping timetables and other people. Our preparations involved packing the back of the pickup with provisions and gear rather than making reservations and drawing up itineraries. We didn't suffer privation or a lack of creature comforts—we ate well and slept in relative comfort on foam mattresses and boat cushions rather than thin backpacker's pads—but the point was to get away. Developed campgrounds, outhouses, campers, and charcoal briquettes were objects of scorn. Crowds were to be avoided at all costs.

I suspect that my father viewed the landscapes of the national park system as sacrifice zones, once-beautiful country given over to paved roads, parking lots, visitor centers, and other accommodations for the mob. As a young man in the early 1960s, he worked for the U.S. Forest Service in southwestern Colorado. Having built quite a few logging roads into the backcountry, he enjoyed intimate knowledge of portions of the San Juan Mountains. He hunted elk and deer on their slopes, fished their river valleys, and when it came time to take his family camping, that's where he headed.

Equating a dearth of people with good times was an impulse compounded by the fact that I had grown up at the edge of Durango, Colorado, a town supported primarily by tourism. As teenagers, my friends and I cultivated a particular brand of contempt for out-of-town visitors, openly exhibiting our disdain for women in pantsuits and gaudy sunglasses, for portly men wearing black socks with their shorts and loafers, for anyone strolling down Main Street with a camera draped around his or her neck.

My arrogance began to fray during college, when I started traveling on my own. Although I hated feeling like a tourist, it dawned on me that this would be the price I would have to pay if I wanted to see and experience new places. I was also no longer close to familiar old campsites and fishing spots and drove a series of aging vehicles with reliability issues and a distinct lack of ground clearance, which limited my adventurousness. When it came time to explore Colorado and Utah with my then-boyfriend from England, parks and monuments were obvious destinations: beautiful, cheap, and uniquely American. Later, after I had met Doug, travel emerged as a favorite mutual pastime. A methodical planner, he assumed the role of in-house travel agent fairly quickly and, lacking my familial bias against national parks, used them as navigation points in our journeys together: Canyonlands, Arches, Island in the Sky; Dinosaur National Monument, Craters of the Moon, Glacier, Canada's Banff, Yellowstone, Grand Teton; Capitol Reef, Bryce Canyon, Grand Staircase–Escalante, Death Valley, Sequoia, Yosemite; Carlsbad Caverns, Guadalupe Mountains, Big Bend. I enjoyed exploring new territory and learned to accept the parks as their own peculiar category of landscape, a hybrid of development and wildness, an inevitable mix of people, vehicles, and natural wonders. Crowds could certainly press, but a five-minute walk would usually leave most of them behind.

My deepening relationship with Doug was also teaching me some of the finer points of compromise. I had first stayed a night in a designated campground when I was in my twenties and had a hard time calling the experience camping. Listening to strangers' lives—beer cans hissing open; people talking, laughing, and snoring; the flush of toilets and squeal of door hinges coming from the restroom bunker—so near at hand yet without solid walls to muffle the sounds was worse than being in one of my cheap college apartments. But I had to accept the fact that if I wanted to camp with Doug, New Jersey–born and possessed of a strong preference for the convenience of indoor plumbing, a developed campground would be involved most of the time.

• • •

Some years into our relationship, Doug and I traveled to California on one of our big road trips. Our ultimate destination was Yosemite, but along the way we visited Capitol Reef, Grand Staircase–Escalante, Bryce Canyon, Death Valley, and Sequoia. Despite the two-week current of sensory input leading up to our arrival in the Yosemite Valley, the landscape did not fail to impress. My eyes, mountain-calibrated though they were, struggled to take in the scale of these novel surroundings. Our campsite afforded a view of Half Dome framed by evergreen boughs, and I enjoyed watching the duet of light and stone playing over the face throughout the day. Looking up at the improbable cliffs and domes from the valley floor, or peering off them from above, the concept of deep geologic time took on a whole new meaning to me. Aside from the outrageous scale of the terrain, there was something peculiar about the place, and I eventually realized that it was the valley's right angles: valleys, in my experience, were V-shaped notches, not squared off like a box.

But if Yosemite impressed me with its geologic grandiosity, it also proved memorable for less charming reasons. There were nightly rounds of applause when RV generators finally fell quiet. The whining, banging, grinding, and thumping of trash trucks woke us at dawn. I felt queasy after I walked to Curry Village and discovered not just the expected gift-and-grocery store, bicycle rental stand, and collection of cabins and tents, but also a mall-sized parking lot, pizza joint, ice cream parlor, bar, and swimming pool. Navigating these "improvements" put my stomach in the kind of clench usually reserved for urban settings.

The culture of bear-proofing was also highly unsettling. Throughout the park, flyers and signs warned that Yosemite's bears had been known to break into cars not just for potato chips and peanut butter, but to get at cans, bottles, baby seats, shampoo, lotion, sunscreen, lip balm, and solitary sticks of gum. These bears, the handouts chided, had learned to recognize ice chests by sight and would break into a car to get at anything that even resembled one. After a day or two, I felt harassed and depressed by the incessant warnings that my carelessness could result in either a ticket or a bear being put to death.

I was also depressed by the kids. Children at Yosemite seemed to do all the same things they would do in any suburban neighborhood: they played noisy games of street soccer, they rode bikes and skateboards on the paved roads looping through the campground, they walked their leashed dogs, they chased one another with water guns equipped with electronic noisemakers. After dark they disappeared, along with their parents, many to be enveloped by the shadowed blue light of televisions flickering inside campers and RVs.

I didn't see any kids out exploring, although with warnings about bears on every available surface, I couldn't blame the parents for not wanting their offspring to be wandering off on their own. And, truth be told, the area around the campgrounds offered little in the way of territory to explore. By virtue of long use and sheer numbers, the campsites stood on barren ground: worn out and picked clean. No grass, no twigs or boughs, no dandelions, not even cheatgrass. No bugs other than flies, no birds other than a flock of shiny black grackles patrolling for crumbs and a few mallards paddling along the barren and eroded banks of the river. Aside from scavenging chipmunks, I didn't see any mammals, not even a bear looking for an ice chest to break into. The lower end of the campground, damaged during floods in 1997, sprouted grass and shrubs but was blocked off with plastic yellow warning tape and "Keep Out" signs. More signs at the edge of the nearby meadow directed us to a raised boardwalk: keep off the grass. The place was more tightly regulated than a city park.

Walking across the boardwalk one afternoon, we passed a park ranger giving a nature talk to a group of kids sitting in a circle on the grass. The privilege of this intimacy with the meadow's flora seemed lost on them; their expressions were of late-afternoon classroom boredom. That's what it's come to, I thought. Summer school. Nature as extra credit.

• • •

Rocky Mountain National Park is an easy drive from the Front Range towns I lived in after college, and for a number of years it served as a reliable destination for day trips with out-of-state visitors. The park provided the requisite grand mountain vistas, easy hiking trails for those without sturdy boots, and a high probability of spotting wildlife. I was unlikely to get the car stuck and could easily locate pretty picnic spots or bathrooms on an as-needed basis. A drive up Trail Ridge Road with a few short hikes along the way satisfied the unspoken duty I felt, as a mountain dweller, to show off the high country to flatlanders.

A few days after my friend Lisa arrived on her first trip to visit me from Texas, that's where we headed. We were both trying to improve our camera skills at the time and were on the lookout for likely photographic subjects. I insisted on taking her to the Alluvial Fan, a feature created when the earthen dam that had held back the waters of Lawn Lake burst on the night of July 15, 1982. The flood regurgitated a raw delta of sediment, boulders, and trees onto the valley floor with a violence still palpable years after the water drained away.

When I first saw it, the Alluvial Fan was a relatively new feature on the landscape, maybe two years old. The scar was abrupt and shocking: an agglomeration of broken boulders and sandy earth. Each stone had been scoured clean of moss or lichen, all greenery buried. Trunks of dead trees jutting from under huge rocks or lying at crazy angles were the only sign that living things had once been anchored to the hillside. On my first walk into the wreckage, a single step carried me across the border between living meadow and shattered ground, from woodland to lifeless jumble, but time has soothed the rawness of the gash. Pine needles and cottonwood leaves from the surrounding area have lodged in crevices and come to rest under the blank rocks, offering a foothold for blowing seeds. Willows, sedges, grasses, and wildflowers have begun to colonize the area, punctuating barren earth with dots and exclamation points of greenery. The margins of the scar have softened, and the air of desolation that once lingered there is fading. The landscape still speaks loud and clear of destruction, but nowadays it also offers quiet commentary on regeneration and continuity.

We parked in the lot on the east side of the alluvium and headed up the trail with our camera gear. Before the asphalt pathway began its meanders among the boulders and tree trunks strewn by the floodwaters, I saw the marmot. The fat brown lump of animal was doing what marmots do, which is not much: sitting on top of a boulder, placidly watching the grassy shimmer of the valley floor.

We stopped, unslung our cameras, stepped off the trail, and started framing our shots. Lisa, lacking a telephoto lens, began creeping closer to our quarry. The marmot pivoted on its perch to watch her step-by-slow-step approach, but it stayed put. At the end of several minutes of patient stalking, she had reached a patch of willow, and the marmot's limits. It cocked its elbows, ready to scurry off the rock. She stopped, stood still, and waited for the animal to relax, while I snapped some pictures of their standoff.

At that point, a family started up the trail from the parking lot. The father carried a little boy, maybe two years old, on his shoulders, and the mother followed more slowly, lugging another youngster strapped into a baby carrier. The father-son unit drew closer to where I stood just off the trail. Dad glanced at me, at Lisa, and, I can only assume, at the dark brown marmot prominently topping the light gray boulder like a cherry on a sundae.

I expected the man to point out the animal to the small human on his shoulders. Maybe he would caution the boy to be quiet, so the lady could get her photo.

Instead, he hoisted the child off his shoulders, plunked him footfirst on the trail, and announced in a firm father-to-toddler voice, "I can't carry you the whole way. You'll have to walk."

The little boy started to whimper. The father headed up the trail again, dragging the child by one arm; the whimpers escalated to piercing wails. Both the marmot and Lisa shifted uneasily, but held their ground. The mother drew even with me and threw a grim glance in my direction. She passed without saying a word. A hundred yards up the trail, just before it curved out of sight, the father picked up the squealing boy. The family disappeared, but the toddler's cries faded more slowly. Lisa carefully raised her camera, bagged a close-up of the marmot, and backed out of the willows. The marmot's idle stare followed her retreat.

"What the heck was that about?" she asked, putting her camera back in her bag.

I shrugged. "I don't know . . . not wanting to look like an indulgent parent in front of us? But I don't see why he had to stir up a scene right here. And they weren't interested in the marmot at all." I put my own camera away, adjusted my daypack, and started up the trail. "Maybe they just assumed that if it was something they were supposed to notice, there would have been a sign pointing it out to them."

. . .

My reaction to the family at the Alluvial Fan shows that I have not entirely shed my adolescent quickness with a sneer, but there's genuine exasperation behind the snide impulse. In a society in which it has become so rare to venture out into a part of the world that has not been shaped exclusively by human whim, desire, or carelessness, why not seize the opportunity when it presents itself? Why bother to get out of the car—why pay the fees and pass through the gate—if not to pay attention, to get a feel for the nuances of where you are?

Wisecracking that those parents weren't interested in the marmot because there was no interpretive sign directing their attention thereto was cheap entertainment for Lisa and me. Disengaged from the moment, it's easier to summon more generous interpretations. Maybe that couple was simply too car-and-kid weary to care. Maybe the father didn't want to call attention to the animal because he just wanted to walk and figured the child would make a scene by wanting to pet the stuffed-looking creature. Maybe they were sick to death of seeing marmots that day: chunky animals that look like giant rats, lolling on boulders all over the park. Perhaps they were appalled at the insensitivity of those two women, harassing innocent wildlife with their cameras. Or they were trying to leave the two blond chicks to their clumsy stalking. Maybe they just wanted to get up the trail to see the landmark promised by roadside signage. Perhaps they were seeking the creek, hustling to immerse themselves in the white noise of water tumbling over boulders at the behest of gravity. It's also possible they weren't interested in the marmot because they hadn't seen it.

Since I became a park visitor late in life, during my inquisitive college years, I seem to be particularly sensitive to the notion of purpose as it applies to this unique category of landscape. Observing the reaction of strangers to the park environment—indifference, astonishment, boredom, cluelessness, quiet awe, or loud proclamations of how the government should be running things differently—provides an added dimension to my own experience. Along with taking in the feel of a place, I watch my fellow visitors and study exhibits on subjects I ostensibly know a fair bit about. I eavesdrop on conversations and even (I imagine my father's eyes rolling) occasionally participate in guided tours and walks, half of my brain listening, half parsing the experience for the messages, implicit and explicit, I'm meant to glean. In short, in addition to exploring unknown places for myself, my visits to national parks have become inquiries into the philosophical terrain of collective expectation.

If the parks are to be perceived, managed, and used as a public resource, what do we, as the public, as users, intend to gain? I'm not particularly comfortable with the notion that these landscapes—or any landscape, for that matter—must be "good" for something, that land must earn its keep on *our* terms. There is a level at which the expectation that we will exit a park having been either emotionally moved or newly informed is yet one more expression of an oversized appetite for gratification. Still, why visit one of the almost four hundred park units across the country? Visitors' expectations can be anticipated somewhat in the case of those places designated as historic sites, battlefields, parkways, and recreational areas, but what of the iconic parks, those massive preserves dedicated to natural landscapes and wildlife? The legislative act that authorized the formation of the National Park Service in 1916 stated that the parks were intended "to conserve the scenery and the natural and historic objects and the wild life therein and to provide for the enjoyment of the same in such manner and by such means as will leave them unimpaired." A more pithy mission statement offered on its modern-day website states, "The National Park Service cares for special places saved by the American people so that all may experience our heritage." The problem is that these phrases reflect the mission of the parks from an administrative standpoint and do not suggest what they mean from a visitor's point of view.

And the fact is that people visit the parks for a variety of reasons: to get a whiff of history, to clean city-clogged respiratory pipes with some fresh air, to feed a pair of eyeballs hungry for the sight of nonengineered landscapes, to feel a little swell of national pride or the contraction of humility. Parks (sometimes) furnish a break from traffic on road trips, but more reliably they offer restrooms, souvenir shops, and nice views to go with a sandwich. Park visitors participate in the Great American Photo Safari: drive, stop, pose, shoot, drive on, share the requisite trophy photo. We like to be able to join the "been-there-done-that" chorus—which is not purely a matter of bragging. In a country as culturally and topographically diverse as the USA, public lands serve as coin in the currency of communal experience: Yellowstone and the Grand Canyon are, like Super Bowl commercials, something we can talk about with people we've never met before. Besides, taking the kids to a national park is cheaper than taking them to Disneyland—in some cases even cheaper than taking them to a movie.

More specifically, though, I suspect it's fair to say that there's a profound associative link between the nation's scenic parks and the concept of "nature" in the minds of many Americans. Although it's simplistic, it's not completely nutty to characterize the scenic parks as ambassadors for the natural world: gifted and charismatic representatives charged with maintaining diplomatic relations between the citizenry of an increasingly urbanized society and the land. The scenic parks offer access to portions of the undeveloped, not-carpentered, unplugged, nonvirtual world to a population increasingly disconnected from the outdoors.

This fact is fairly obvious and not inconsequential, but the diplomatic analogy masks a pretty appalling situation. If national parks are representatives of nature (trammeled or otherwise), and if they exist as dedicated set-asides within well-defined boundaries, then we run the risk of redefining "nature" as a set of geographic locations rather than the biological, meteorological, geological, and climatological matrix in which our species exists at all times and as a matter of life and death. Add to this the idea that the natural world we live in—the very foundation, framework, and lifeblood of human existence—requires a diplomatic corps and you have a pretty sad commentary on the state of our culture. Surely we should take as bizarre and terrifying the possibility that many of us equate the environment on which our very lives depend with tourist attractions.

Then there's the possibility that the national parks provide excuses for continuing excess. Park holdings offer the comfortable illusion that we have, as a society, paid our dues to the natural world: the grandeur, open spaces, and habituated wildlife on display induce a sense of abundance, of ecological richness and health. Canadian writer Kevin Van Tighem frames this tendency as a moral hazard. In *Coming West,* he asserts bluntly that instead of drawing us into a more thoughtful relationship with our habitat, formal parklands have "encouraged us to embrace an approach to conservation that consists mostly of trading large protected areas in exchange for the freedom to abuse all other land." Rather than counteracting the impulse to view our technological society as operating beyond the reach of natural law, the existence of parks as set-asides and preserves may simply reinforce our worst environmental habits.

Aligning the scenic parks with an ideal of nature and sheltering them with fences or overly restrictive rules risks turning them into museums and zoos, places where people are expected to look but not to touch. Emphasizing boundaries and venerating the pristine perpetuates the false notion that nature is a place that has little to do with our day-to-day lives. There is a sense in which championing the qualities that make parklands unique and special feeds the vicious cycle of binary thinking that positions paired concepts—people/nature, built/wild, damaged/protected—in terms of opposition and conflict rather than complementarity and mutual dependence.

Such matters are certainly more philosophical than practical. Idealizing the pristine might complicate some people's understanding of the natural order, but by far the biggest issue for park managers is crowd control. Millions of visitors arrive at the parks every year, bringing with them a sense of entitlement to paved roads on which to drive their private automobiles, to flush toilets, to gift shops, to entertaining displays, to cell phone service, and to the sense that Uncle Sam is looking out for their safety.

At the time we were in Sequoia National Park, cabins and other buildings that had been built at the base of the magnificent trees were being removed. Signs posted on the fences surrounding the deconstruction zones advised visitors that soil compaction and altered hydrology from the buildings and concentrated human activities had been killing the trees. Like abandoning the practice of feeding Yellowstone's black bears garbage and barring private cars from the road into Zion Canyon during peak season, such changes reflect a management philosophy that places the needs of the parks' native denizens in front of the wishes of human visitors. Making restoration initiatives an explicit part of the park experience opens up the possibility that more visitors might recognize that preserving the well-being of the "natural world" may require actual effort on the part of humanity and will even, conceivably, require sacrifice and self-control on the part of individuals.

As it turns out, their weird hybrid character as preserves run through by development puts scenic parks and wildlife refuges in the position of teaching people who live in cities or the fake pastoralism of suburbia something about the complex relationships between developed and undeveloped landscapes. What better demonstration of the diffuse effects of industrialism than the Grand Canyon on a bad air day? Don't Yosemite's bears make an excellent case for the argument that "wild" is not an absolute? Aren't the battered campgrounds and traffic jams of Yosemite an apt illustration of the pressures of population growth within the bounds of finite geographical space?

Education wasn't mentioned in the parks' enabling legislation. This isn't a surprise, given that the majority of the nation's population in 1916 lived in rural settings. Dirt, weather, livestock, and wild animals were part of everyday life. The relationships between land and food on the table and water in the basin were explicit. For most people, satisfying basic needs required daily effort in the outdoors. Back then, who could have imagined that the largest portion of the American public would see wild animals through the filters of cartoon parables, fenced zoos, and television documentaries? Who could have foreseen the radical distancing of the population from the cycles of production that carry food, water, clothing, and shelter to the local supermarket, mall, and home improvement center?

The National Park Service deserves credit for initiatives to educate visitors about the ecosystems in its holdings. The agency also strives to articulate the interdependencies between parklands and the larger social and ecological frameworks beyond their borders. These efforts are honorable, but they aren't without complications. In the context of our relentless consumer age, I can't help but wonder whether we are poised on the brink where environmental education becomes yet one more commodity, another case in which "nature" is reduced to a resource available for extraction, purchase, and/or exploitation. We approach this edge very closely when the implicit lesson to visitors is that learning about marmots requires buying a DVD or attending a nature talk or playing an interactive game on a computer rather than sitting down on a rock and watching one.

The tendency to defer to expert knowledge and teaching has its roots in good intentions: we listen to what experts have to say because we admire specialized knowledge and are sometimes capable of admitting that we don't, personally, know absolutely everything. So, what could possibly be wrong with consulting a ranger or a placard to learn about that marmot? For one thing, the desire to easily access information (preferably in a condensed and unambiguous form) easily morphs into sensory laziness: an unwillingness to simply be present, to open our eyes and shut our mouths, to breathe, to explore, to touch and feel. Deferring to "interpreters" for first impressions, no matter how noble their intentions, invites passivity and has the potential to short-circuit curiosity. "Learning" becomes a matter of memorizing what someone else has decided is relevant or worth knowing, rather than pursuing the convolutions of individual interests, appreciating the serendipity of context, wallowing alone through a bog of ambiguity. Bored disinterest, an absence of critical thinking skills, and brittle fundamentalism are apt to result—and the fact that these same attributes emerge in kids passing through our public education system should not be cited in defense of the approach.

Human beings once gained fluency in the ways of the environment through repeated informal exposures and ongoing explorations of their surroundings: by firsthand observation and imitation and by initiation under the guidance of elders. Awareness of the world around us is the basis for the laudable cognitive prowess of our species. How strange that we have come to view direct sensory experience as unnecessary or less desirable than virtual interactions, that we seem to have lost our faith in environments that are not cleansed or filtered or themed. How odd that so many of us are under the impression that the cognitive skills our brains honed over millions of years need expert supervision to be properly engaged.

The notion that kids, in particular, need to be "inspired" to appreciate nature is an insidious message that denies the inborn capacity of our species to observe and explore our surroundings under our own idiosyncratic cognitive power, but it's also a symptom of a deeper social shift toward indoor lifestyles and controlled childhood experiences. This topic has been articulately mapped by writers such as Gary Paul Nabhan and Stephen Trimble in *The Geography of Childhood* and Richard Louv in *Last Child in the Woods*. These volumes offer far more informed, impassioned, and detailed arguments for allowing (or, if need be, prodding) kids to explore the world beyond the computer screen, outside the walls of home, and beyond the safety-engineered playset than I, as a childless individual, can offer. Their arguments do make me wonder how relevant Junior Ranger programs are to kids who lack the fundamental sensory experience of playing outside in environments that have not been purged of sharp objects, insects, diverse flora, and hard or abrasive surfaces.

As society becomes ever-more dominated by technological distractions and pay-for-fun commercialism, I realize just how profoundly lucky I am to have spent those hours and days and nights outside when I was young, when the smell of spruce trees and the curve of slickrock underfoot and the smear of the Milky Way on a clear night, viewed from a dew-damp pillow, could be printed indelibly onto the fabric of my being. Because of this personal history, I'm more comfortable in the rumpled woodlands of the central Rockies than in any city on earth, am oddly soothed by spare and bristly landscapes of piñon and sage run through with arroyos. Walking into a desert landscape fills my atheistic bones with peace.

My family headed to the woods or to the shores of nearby desert reservoirs to camp in part because that's what my father—a force of nature in himself—wanted to do and in part because it was a cheap way for a family of six to vacation. My parents and Cindy weren't bent on enriching the children by exposing them to the natural world; they needed a break from their jobs and everyday routines. They expected us to entertain ourselves, and we did so, both individually and as a group. The truck and boat may have been laden with provisions and gear, but there seldom was much in the way of toys or games: a ball, maybe, or a Frisbee if someone remembered to pack one. We kids spent our time exploring, sometimes as a mini-pack, but more often on our own. I recall hours spent poking around under river rocks, flaking the bark of pine trees into separate curvy puzzle pieces, painstakingly trying to create building blocks or wheels from compacted clumps of sand. My brother Doug and I built miniature buildings from twigs, mud, and rocks. We played house in the small caves cut by the wind into Navajo sandstone or given shape by groves of gambel oak or the sprawled branches of fallen trees.

I treasure those experiences and value the foundations they've provided for my adult proclivities for observation and musings about natural history, but it didn't occur to me that they might be unusual until I began to encounter people for whom "nature" was foreign territory, for whom spending time outside without turf grass or grandstand seating or smoothly finished sidewalks was far out of the ordinary. I've accumulated many memories and photographs from the national parks over the past twenty-odd years, but ultimately the value of those visits has been in how they have deepened my gratitude for my past.

· · ·

The *what for?* of paying a visit to one of our nation's national parks is, in the end, deeply personal, but it emerges from an ancient and pervasive human impulse: to explore the world, to see and smell and touch and hear it for ourselves. By means of an epic road trip, a package vacation, or a spontaneous detour off a familiar road, we remove ourselves from the everyday. Nowadays, travel is hyped to be all about shopping, going off a diet, partying, expanding a hoard of souvenirs, or adding to a lifelist of been-there-done-that, but the inborn pursuit of curiosity is still in there: taking a journey entails exposing our brains to the novelty of different places and the presence of people from outside the familial group.

In deliberately exposing ourselves to that which is different, we shake up our comfortable norms and routines, and when circumstances align, we crack ourselves open a bit. It might take some time and reflection, but sometimes we wind up confronting the limits of one or two of our assumed truths.

As Lisa and I strolled the path through the Alluvial Fan in Rocky Mountain National Park that day, we passed the family we had encountered earlier. The little boy was sliding down a small section of water-polished rock while his dad watched. The kid was having a great time, and I hoped that the father was thinking about something other than the fact that the boy was getting his pants dirty.

The mother was sitting not far away, the infant carrier near her elbow. She seemed to be resting, enjoying a respite between stints in the car with two young children. Perhaps she was cultivating thoughtfulness, immersing herself in the moment. Feeling the contours of the rock beneath her, the sun on her face. Letting the rumble of water pass through her body, allowing the wind to comb her hair on its way to the pine forests beyond the alluvium. Contemplating some aspect of the landscape that I hadn't even noticed.

Modern Frontier

From our house tucked in the foothills west of Boulder, I could be downtown in fifteen minutes. I was content to be a homebody even then, but this is proving to be a particularly useful trait now that we've moved to our new home place, located just east of Colorado's center point. From here, it takes ten minutes just to get to a paved road, and then it's still some twenty-five miles to Cañon City, which is the nearest sizable town. The hamlet of Guffey (population thirty-four, they say) is a mere twelve miles away, but that's mostly on dirt roads, so the trip takes a half hour each way in good weather. Once there, my options are limited: Guffey lacks a grocery store, hardware store, or even, rather strikingly in Twenty-first Century America, a gas station, although it does have a post office. Since the postal service regards our area as too rural for a rural delivery route, I make the drive to Guffey once a week to pick up mail from our PO box.

You don't move to a place like this if you're addicted to pizza delivered to your front door or if you need to jump-start your day with a latte served up by a chirpy barista. There's no popping to the store if you're missing an ingredient for something you want to cook. We make our own pizza, buy tea in bulk, plan meals ahead, keep a well-stocked pantry, and sometimes just make do without.

In exchange for the fleeting conveniences of fast food and home delivery of bills and junk mail, we enjoy the privilege of living in a place where, no matter which direction we look, there is either a dramatic long-distance view or an intricate foreground mosaic of flora and stone. The neighbors who are furred or scaly or feathered outnumber people by a crazy ratio.

We owned this property for five years before beginning our move away from Boulder. During that time, we came down to camp and hike when we could fit it in. We would talk about where we'd put a house and what it might be like to live up here. Back then, the main county road wasn't fully paved, and the last leg of our journey required stopping to open and close several stock gates. Our property had a rough road scraped to the top of the ridge where we would camp, but no power, no water well. We listened to elk bugling in the fall, nighthawks diving in the summer. Coyotes discovering our camp yipped and yodeled in protest.

In the spring of 2001, we began the move from Boulder, renting a house in Guffey while we built a barn with a small cabin attached to it. That December, with the cabin complete and the house in Fourmile Canyon sold, we stored most of our stuff in the shell that would eventually be the horse barn and settled in to the four-hundred-square-foot cabin.

Aside from a patch of tile in the bathroom kept toasty by in-floor heat, the cabin is warmed only by a small woodstove, so chopping kindling and keeping the firewood box stacked full were urgent chores last winter, as was running the snowplow. At eighty-nine hundred feet in elevation, the winter in these parts is long and features unfriendly temperatures, shoving winds, low-slung clouds, and the early closure of night's lid. We walked after dinner now and again, but did so in the dark and weren't apt to dawdle. Going outside required the intermediate process of putting on boots, coat, gloves, and a hat or scarf, but even then the transition between the warm air of indoors and the chill outside was harsh. Before heading to the post office I would throw a shovel and my snow boots in the car, just in case.

Now that summer is upon us, I no longer need to bundle up to fend off the wind and cold, although the sun's rays are so intense at this elevation that I still don a hat and gloves when I go outside. Visitors exclaim about the expansive views and ask us whether we know how lucky we are. In the colder months our guests were more rare, and while they would comment on the scenery, they were more focused on access, asking, in edgy voices, how bad the roads get, and don't we feel isolated?

The roads do get bad, and since we're more than a mile from a county-maintained road and have to plow ourselves out when they do, I've become highly attentive to weather. Rather than being a drawback, though, I consider the paucity of human neighbors to be a bonus. I am stunned and thrilled daily: what a wonder to find myself living in a place that fosters my senses with beauty, stillness, and the occasional jolts of an extreme environment. Every day, my attention is called outward, away from self-involvement. I feel more self-reliant and am more keenly aware of my surroundings, not only because they are pretty, but because many of the buffers that modern life usually places between me and the world are stripped away. Living close to the bellies of thunderclouds, with their stabbing branches of lightning, for example, forces me to pattern my days according to the rhythm of afternoon thunderstorms: one of my primary chores at the moment is gathering rocks for the raised beds that we're building in the garden. This task needs to be done early in the day; thunderstorms start to rumble their warnings that I should be off the ridgetop soon after lunch.

The rural setting also obliges me to acquire and apply skills that are irrelevant to a life in town. Although we're not ranchers, we live in ranch country and are surrounded by open range. Cattle are a regular presence in our lives. I've learned to keep a sharp eye out for calves that are acting playful near the roadside, and although a rancher in a tall truck would guffaw at my fastidiousness, I consider it adaptive behavior to steer around cow pies on the road. Fresh manure will paint the side skirts of my low-slung car, and if it's winter and the pile is frozen, the shock to my wheels is no different from hitting a rock.

In short, I feel like I've sidestepped the modern trend toward ease and convenience. Chopping wood for heat, plowing the roads ourselves, building a garden from the materials at hand, staying alert for changes in the weather: there's a distinct frontier flair to it all.

I'd be a fool, though, to pretend that my life here is anything other than thoroughly modern. Not so many years ago, building a house on the site we've picked would have branded us as unsuspecting tenderfoots. Homesteaders settling in this area around the turn of the last century built compact houses near surface water, nestled in hollows where they would be protected from the wind. Selecting a house site for the views it affords no longer verges on naïve lunacy, but this decision, along with the choice to move to this remote place when we're neither independently wealthy nor planning on securing our living from the land, could hardly be more new-fashioned. Our location might pose challenges that invite references to the past, but we wouldn't be able to live here at all if it weren't for a variety of technological advances that make ours the very antithesis of a frontier life.

I'm lucky enough to work from home, but my productivity depends on an Internet connection. Since Doug is not a miner or a rancher—the traditional means of making a living in these parts—he commutes to his job. The drive is long and requires looking out for deer, elk, and free-range cattle crossing the road, along with all the weather-related hazards you'd expect from a mountain environment. An all-wheel-drive car, good tires, and paved roads make it possible, though, even if the practice is not environmentally friendly.

The technologies behind work and transportation are only the most superficial examples of the modern wonders that support our lifestyle. Even if an early rancher had wanted to build on a rocky and windswept ridge for some reason, logistical issues would have been a major deterrent. Laying a road on such ground required big incentives in the past: the promise of more fertile and gentle land beyond, or valuable ore dug from the mountainside. Nowadays, a pretty view offers sufficient enticement.

I might feel plucky when I'm chopping kindling to light the woodstove, but let's face it: we hauled the wood in with a pickup truck driven on a road I didn't have to lift a finger to build. Instead, a backhoe carved our driveway into the side of the ridge in a day, and a dump truck followed with gravel road base to smooth out the track. Plowing the road ourselves has demanded that we learn a whole new style of driving said pickup, but the cab is heated and the hydraulics of the plow operate with a switch. I might be building the garden's raised beds by hand, but we're leaving the job of digging the foundation for our house to a big diesel-powered excavator that methodically bites the hillside away in chunks.

Our water comes from a well drilled by a specialized rig and is drawn from the depths by an electric pump. A small wood-burning stove is more than adequate for heating our little cabin, thanks in large part to the high-tech insulation within its walls. We'll burn wood from local trees in the house, too, but will rely primarily on a radiant heating system. The added bonus of passive solar heating will be made possible by windows engineered to be thermally efficient: large enough to usher in lots of sun (and nice views) without freezing us out at night.

We're not survivalists seeking escape from a threatening world. We're not pursuing a subsistence lifestyle, eating only what we can forage or hunt or grow on our land. We're not adventurers nor antisocial misfits. We're not farmers (in this climate, I'll consider whatever we grow for the dinner table a minor victory), and we're not ranchers, either. If we slack off on our chores around the place, we won't starve or go belly up.

Drawn to this place by the beauty of the rucked and grass-clad land, the sky, the animals and birds, and the opportunity to focus on building a life together, we're working at building that life using all the tools at our disposal: hands and imagination as well as technology and power tools. We're working hard to create a solid and efficient house and to cultivate a lifestyle that's modest and honors the local conditions as much as possible. The modern conveniences that ease our lives here are not necessarily the same ones that most urban and suburban residents would call amenities, but to deny our reliance on them would be both a lie and an ingratitude.

The spiral of the seasons has brought summer upon us. The warm air and promise of wildflowers lure me outside, where self-congratulation is irrelevant. The finest attributes of this place are the ones for which I can claim no responsibility. There's a sense of opulence in these long days, with plenty of time after dinner for a leisurely sunset walk. Chores that don't get finished one day can be picked up the next. The windows are open to breezes scented by sage and yarrow. I walk in and out of the cabin without much thought about the shelter its margins provide. Town is a long way away, but distance is one of the luxuries we moved here to enjoy. We were fortunate to have found this place, are lucky to be able to afford to make the leap toward the vision of what our lives might be in such a place. I might not be a hearty frontier woman, but I am in the process of becoming a more grateful human being.

Tyranny of the Visible

"Wow. Great view."

The comment is almost inevitable when someone who has never been to our place arrives, be they a visitor or contractor or even someone from the area stopping by for the first time.

"Yes," I say, trying to sound both humble and grateful, "we're very spoiled."

The visitor is usually faced northeast from the house site, admiring Pikes Peak looming at the horizon like an archetype of mountain-ness. Emerging from the surrounding terrain with a conical form—albeit rather squished—the mountain's broad base is cloaked with the blackish hue of conifers, a pretty contrast with the purple-gray of its summit. Winter snows polish the peak to a white gleam, creating a canvas for alpenglow in the lingering light of cold evenings.

Proximity, bulk, and its isolated position—a lone eminence without a range of fellows to keep it company—make Pikes an authoritative visual draw, but the drama of the vista is largely due to our position up on a sizable ridge overlooking High Park, a grassy pan that lies between here and the mountain. Just below the house, pine and fir crowd the steep slope of the ridge, which falls some five hundred vertical feet to an array of rocky drainages wandering across dozens of acres, widening here and there into small meadows. Clusters of gambel oak and dark junipers dot the jumble of stone and grass. In the middle distance, High Park shimmers, usually tanned to the color of a buckskin horse but softly green in a wet spring or after a few summer thunderstorms. Beyond High Park, granite outcrops rise as conifer-darkened foothills and pucker into drainages at the southwestern foot of Pikes Peak.

As dramatic and appealing as this view is, I actually prefer the outlook to the north. Less spectacular but more striking, this line of sight also leads the eye first down and then back up. The features of the terrain have a fluidity that's anomalous for the mountains, though, bulging and swooping instead of jutting. These formations are the weathered remains of the Thirtynine Mile and Cripple Creek volcanic fields, which dominated the area for several million years starting around thirty-four million years ago. Layer upon layer of ash, lava, pyroclastic flows, and the jumbled debris of lahar flows spilled over the more ancient granite intrusions. As the volcanic deposits eroded over time, patches of resistant materials created protective caps that became the buttes, tablelands, cones, and flat-topped ridges visible today. The view toward Pikes Peak is what you might expect of the central Rockies of Colorado, while this northerly panorama is an unexpected eruption of plains geography.

Either aspect is charming, and the views in other directions aren't shabby, either. The ridge we're on splits just west of here; the grassy trough between the crests of high ground will make a nice horse pasture someday. The horizon to the southwest is dominated by a higher swell of land called Cap Rock Ridge. The flat summit toward its eastern end calls to mind a massive barge caught broadside on a turfy wave. The ground falls away from Cap Rock's prow to create a concave frame for the long-distance view, which includes the dark ripple of the Wet Mountains and the jagged peaks of the Sangre de Cristos.

I'd be lying if I said that the visual charm of the place didn't woo us when we were looking for property outside of Boulder. Spooked by a neighboring property owner engaged in an enormous building project under unorthodox zoning circumstances and lured by the prospect of eventually keeping horses, we had looked at dozens of properties across Colorado before we found our way to this peculiar archipelago of ridges nestled in the center of the state. The land's rolling pelt of grass and scattering of trees drew us in with its visual charms, but it also met our more pragmatic criteria for pasturage and affordability. We signed a contract for the land the day after we first saw it.

Our move to Cap Rock Ranch reinvigorated my self-assigned task of observing my surroundings with new flora, novel terrain, more wildlife, a wider view. The twist of red on a late-summer blade of grass might catch my eye one moment, the crazed flight of a Say's phoebe pursuing a fly the next. I watch the tops of thunderheads flaring with interior light on summer afternoons, admire the sculpted brows of snowdrifts in winter. Having the time to dally and a home range in which to do so is a double privilege, and I do what I can to make the best of it.

Besides, watching is easy: using my eyes is a matter of doing what comes naturally.

Human beings have neither the sharpest nor the most refined eyesight in the animal kingdom, but we are profoundly visual creatures. Neurologists mapping brain function have implicated as much as 70 percent of the human brain in activities that make use of visual input. This isn't to say that a majority of our brainpower is dedicated exclusively to processing things we're seeing. Instead, the human brain has made an art of co-opting the information delivered to it via the optic nerves. News arriving along those conduits is merged with input from the other senses. Visual information is reused and recombined to foster higher brain functions we don't much associate with seeing, such as memory and abstract thinking.

Language reflects this cognitive bias toward the visual. English is so thoroughly laced with terms that are related to the act of seeing (*perception, appearance, observe, visionary, point of view, focus, perspective, resemble, worldview, witness, outlook, lookout, wait and see, don't you see?*) that having a conversation without using such phrases, while certainly possible, requires operating under a handicap. Try telling a friend a story about an exciting event that happened over the weekend without using the words *saw, watched,* or *looked like*, without relying on terms that allow you to convey color or shape or speed of movement. *You should have seen it!* you might say, or *It was the damnedest thing I've ever seen!* To which your friend, skeptical, might reply, *I'll believe it when I see it.*

Aspiring writers are hounded to *show, don't tell* in the interest of engaging the imagination of the reader. The idea is to mine the text with descriptive tripwires that will ignite interior images, trigger memories, evoke association and empathy. Nouns and verbs, adjectives and adverbs, metaphor and simile—these parts of speech and literary devices give energy and texture to a flat code of letters. Such devices aren't effective because of any inherent quality—they're just words, after all—but because they have the potential to coax the reader's mind to join in a cognitive dance with the text. To say that I live in a pretty place amounts to offering my opinion to an unknown reader. To attempt a description of what I see around me is an invitation to that stranger to begin to see the world the way I do.

Our eyes are not mere passive peepholes. They function as couriers in negotiations between an individual and the external world. Seeing is a connective process, a matter of letting the world in. Grotesque but revealing experiments on kittens conducted in the 1960s showed that if one eye was stitched shut for the first six months of the animal's life, the cat would be blind in that eye. Structurally, the eye was normal, but connections between it and the brain failed to develop in the absence of stimulation. Studies of human individuals who had cataracts as children demonstrate similar results. Without visual stimulation during the appropriate developmental phase, brain cells do not link up to form the networks for processing ocular information. Deprived of sensation streaming in from the eyes, the brain co-opts regions normally dedicated to visual processing and uses them for other cognitive functions. The brain of an individual blind from birth is not smaller than that of a sighted person, but it is wired differently.

The development of specialized processing skills is not the only example of the brain's proactive relationship with sensory impulses arriving from the world beyond the skull's bony cup. Neural processes analyze incoming information, making determinations of relevance and significance below the level of conscious thought. Negotiations with a vast and complicated and dynamic world demand a degree of selectivity. One theory accounting for the social withdrawal and ritualized behaviors characteristic of autism is that they are responses to a neural environment in which the filters that usually curtail the influx of raw sensation have failed. For most of us, the clamor of sound that penetrates a city apartment is thus reduced to background noise. We become acclimatized to scents. We do not, as a general rule, perceive the texture and pressure of our clothes against our skin. Similarly, we don't "visualize" every photon that streams into our eyes and interacts with our retinas.

The unconscious editing by which the brain credits some photons with meaningful information and disregards others means that we develop habits of seeing. We cultivate visual expectations, acquire perceptual preferences. We learn to see, in the sense of acquiring the ability to process visual input, as infants, but we continue to learn to see some things and ignore others throughout our lives.

At our previous home in Fourmile Canyon, I got sick and tired of being unable to tell whether the large dark bird soaring over my head was a raven, a raptor, or a vulture. I'd get excited, thinking I was seeing an eagle, and the bird would croak a raven's laugh at me as it tilted out of sight. So I took a class on raptor identification, began studying field guides, and started going out to look for raptors so I could practice my identification skills. This subcategory of birding was ideal for me, since it didn't require getting up in the dark to greet the dawn chorus. A midmorning field trip to the plains east of Boulder would often yield two dozen birds, obligingly perched on telephone poles and bare cottonwoods or hovering over one of the prairie dog colonies on the county's open space. As I learned the field marks that distinguish one bird of prey from another, I got faster at zeroing in on certain body parts so I could make the identification before the bird flew from its perch or shrank to a speck in the binoculars. With practice, I learned how to tell whether a soaring bird was a raven or a golden eagle or a vulture based on body shape and flight behavior alone.

The raptors I now watch for were always there, perched on poles and trees as I traveled the roadways of Colorado over the years. They were hovering and soaring as I rode my horses as a girl and when I went hiking as a young adult. It just took me thirty-five years to learn to notice them.

Sight is not an all-inclusive faculty, although the flow of images streaming into our brains is so captivating that we can be seduced into disregarding limitations that affect what and how well we see. I can extol the stateliness of a venerable Douglas fir, for example, but my admiration is based on my perception of its superficial aspects. The tree's roots twist and curl unseen through soil and rock; beetles tunnel in the wood, invisible beneath the bark. The biomechanics of our eyes dictate that we see in the visible portion of the electromagnetic spectrum, leaving us blind to frequencies at either end. We cannot discern tiny things with the naked eye and are limited in our perception of large ones by temporal and physical forces. Our eyes are tuned to register movement, but we have trouble perceiving objects that move very very fast or judging their motion if it's very very slow. With eyes that are fixed in our heads, our point of view must follow the orientation of our face. Distance, folds in the landscape, and opaque objects that block what lies beyond them all impinge on our already narrow perspective.

The horizon is abundant, our lines of sight limited. Not so long ago I was fantasizing about what it will be like to work in my new office, with windows facing in the four cardinal directions. Picturing myself sitting at my desk, admiring the Cap Rock perpetually chugging along the swell to the south, an image flashed through my mind of a magnificent raptor veering past the north-facing window. Behind my head. Unseen.

A grazing horse does not suffer from this handicap: with their heads lowered, horses can see almost a full 360 degrees around them. Such expanded peripheral vision is common in animals that rely on fleeing rather than fighting for survival. Chameleons and seahorses can rotate their eyes, and crabs and shrimp have their visual organs perched on stalks, giving them a similar advantage. Human beings are visual runts in other ways, too. The sensitive cones that line the backs of our eyes allow us to see color, but we can't see well in the dark like mountain lions, cuttlefish, and owls can. Many insects and arachnids have multiple eyes, and some have compound eyes with thousands of lenses. We honor the visual acuity of birds of prey with the term *eagle eye*, but sharpness of vision is not their only talent. Some species can detect light in the ultraviolet range. Rodent urine left along pathways through grass lights up in UV, so a kestrel hovering over a field sees the terrain as if it were an illuminated map showing the trails used by mice and voles.

• • •

Some fourteen miles away as the raven flies, to the right of Pikes Peak's bald summit as seen from here, there's a long horizontal band of pinkish-gray treeless ground. This is the worksite of the Cripple Creek & Victor Gold Mining Company. You can take in the view of Pikes Peak and not "see" the mine. The raw mountainside in the zone of destruction is paler, but it resembles the weathered stone of the mountain's summit just enough that your eyes can be tricked into believing that timberline has found a reason to pool a thousand feet or two lower in one particular area. Once your eyes tune in to what you're seeing, the bare expanse resolves into an arrangement of long terraces that are clearly made by humans. The physical destruction is obvious and striking. Sometimes, on a snowy day, you can see a dark gray plume spilling over the lip of one of the terraces: debris cascading down the steep slope, dumped from a truck the size of a house. At night, powerful work lights create a yellowed constellation that shifts gradually over the months as operations and piles of rubble move around the site.

People have been extracting gold from this flank of Pikes Peak since the late 1800s. The two towns that lend their names to the modern mine were home to more than forty-five thousand people around 1910, when the richest strikes were being worked. The area was pocked with tailings and lift frames, the ground riddled with shafts and tunnels. Much of that is gone now—not lost on the winds of time so much as blasted away, along with acres of topsoil, grass, trees, and a considerable chunk of the mountainside. Cripple Creek and Victor are tiny towns now, home to only about sixteen hundred people, but the CC&V is a modern operation, which is to say that it's industrial-scale. Explosives fracture the mountainside. Heavy machinery pulverizes the chunks. Gigantic trucks haul and stack the rubble.

Getting closer doesn't add much in the way of detail, although proximity does offer a better impression of the operation's size. Driving the road that winds between Cripple Creek and Victor skirts you along the lower edge of one of the massive terraces, which completely fills your field of view and incites a little prickle of dread at the looming presence of all that no-longer-solid rock.

The excavation scar and terraces are huge and awful, but they don't tell the whole story. Sometimes, using our eyes is more suited to raising a question—*What the hell goes on over there at that mine?*—than answering it. To understand anything other than the enormity of its excavation, I had to do more than look at the mine.

I credit my dad with opening up the natural world to me, but I never would have been able to make much sense of its influence if it hadn't been for the matching gift from my mother, which was a fondness for reading, books, and writing. She signed me up for a book club before I even entered school, and time spent with those slim volumes set me on a lifelong path in which books are companions, diversions, sources of information, repositories of inspiration.

My observational dabbling has blended butt-in-the-chair readerly habits with my amateur field observations. I've gone for walks and sat on a lot of grass and many rocks and logs, but *paying attention* has also involved perusing field guides, memoirs, reports, websites, pamphlets, magazine articles, maps, and books.

Reading up on the CC&V, I learned that the terraces are not the heart of the operation. They're what the mining company calls "overburden storage areas," which consist of the millions of tons of the mountainside that don't bear any ore. The much smaller portion, the ore-bearing material, is sent to the operation's leach facility to be treated with a dilute sodium cyanide solution that dissolves the gold. Captured by a liner laid under the pile, the gold is separated out from the cyanide solution, which is then reused on a fresh pile of ore.

Cyanide: a sinister word, a deadly poison. Yet, cyanide, too, is just one chapter in the bigger story. Blasting millions of tons of rock off the mountain liberates minerals that were once sequestered under the land's surface. Getting to buried deposits is the whole point of mining, of course, but the minerals of interest tend to be mixed with a variety of others. According to the EPA's Toxics Release Inventory, land releases of arsenic, chromium, mercury, and zinc from the CC&V amounted to nearly 31,000 pounds in 2002, the year of our home's construction. That same year, reporting documents show air releases of lead compounds in the amount of 2.8 million pounds.

Compared with cyanide, lead seems pedestrian, a part of my everyday world. I've *seen* lead, touched it. I think of its yielding texture, of the weighty apron draped across my chest and belly when a dental tech takes x-rays of my teeth, of my father biting split shot sinkers closed on a filament of line when rigging my fishing pole when I was young. The terms *pencil lead* and *unleaded gasoline* preserve the material in common vernacular even though we stopped using lead in those products years ago.

Those product formulations changed because lead is a health hazard. Inside the body's envelope, lead passes as counterfeit calcium. Calcium helps nerves trade impulses across synaptic gaps, and when lead takes its place, the legitimate commerce of the nervous system is disrupted. Lead poisoning causes clouded thought and impaired judgment. Commands to the limbs falter, making the afflicted weak or clumsy. Lead also damages the signaling mechanisms that regulate attention and self-control, so that its presence in the human body is linked to ADD, ADHD, degenerate behavior, and violence. Lead's effects on the developing brains of children can be so devastating that no level of exposure is considered safe for them.

The information that is relevant to sodium cyanide solution and lead cannot be determined from looking at a vial of the former or a lump of the latter. Gold is pretty enough, but its appearance doesn't really account for its status in many of the world's civilizations. The history of hard rock mining and gold rushes throughout the West are an undeniable part of the reality of the CC&V, but we grasp the notional less by way of firsthand observation than by the recombinant processes of analyzing evidence and parsing narratives. What's hidden is not the same as that which cannot be discerned by the eye, which is different from that which is insubstantial yet consequential. Visualizing the world depends on what we're capable of seeing and on what we choose to see, but perception also depends on recognizing things we never "see" at all.

· · ·

A stand of evergreens is draped over the hillside below our house site like a dark green apron with a light-colored rick-rack of scrub oak trimming the sides. The conifer woods are thick, and on a windy day (which isn't uncommon up here), I can escape the incessant pushing and the whipping of hair into my eyes, entering an airspace of relative calm, even if the treetops hiss and groan in the turbulence. In the dark timber, winters are lengthy, and even in high summer the shadows are deep. Rocky Mountain maple, mountain spray, and creeping juniper intermix with the fir and spruce, creating a forest more classically woodsy than the ponderosa and grass mix more typical of our area. The evergreens fracture here and there into openings that accommodate stands of aspen or room-sized glens. On the ground, a thick brown carpet of duff is broken up in places with throw rugs woven in the green hues of grass, moss, blue clematis, and wild strawberries.

There's an undeniable loveliness to all these different shadings of woodland ecology. A gentle hike along the game trails laced through the trees, despite the challenges the sidehill poses to my ankles, yields many of the little gifts a walker might hope for: the scuttle and scold of an Abert's squirrel; oval depressions left in the soft earth by bedded elk; rocks tossed lichen-side down by a foraging bear; aspens draped with catkins like dangly earrings in the early spring; the profile of a Clark's nutcracker on her nest; secret mossy grottoes; the scent of damp earth, luxurious in a dry climate.

One of the charms of walking in this area is that I'm away from the barn and the driveway and construction site that is becoming our house. I can avoid looking at the raw earth and the machinery that present unequivocal visual evidence of the consequences of my presence. Walk straight up the hillside from the jackstraw pattern of game trails, however, and before you arrive at the brow of the ridge you'll be faced with the taut parallel lines of a five-strand barbed wire fence. Scattered among the trees are saw-cut stumps and intermittent sections of fencing constructed from small-diameter logs. Walk far enough downslope and you'll hit another fence, with a rutted two-track road just beyond that. Use any of the drainages in the area as a walking path and you'll eventually come across at least one earthen check dam.

My habit is to perceive such evidence of human activity in a landscape that otherwise reads as wild as interruptions or blemishes. This is an old tendency, but its persistence is encouraged by my taste for nature writing. It would seem that there's nothing amiss with an emphasis on those aspects of the universe that are not of human origin in a genre that takes the natural world as its topic, but I've lately begun to wonder. The mine, roads, fence lines, and buildings aren't the most charming aspects of the view from home, but they're part of the reality of my society and of this place. This is not a wilderness area: it is a working landscape, terrain that supports a wildland ecology as well as homes, recreational and ranching activities, and mining. The land is home to animals and plants but also to people and the signs of their passage and history.

Literature cheats physics, providing a solitary individual with the means of seeing, however imperfectly, through someone else's eyes. Written language has allowed the human race to exponentially expand what any single person might learn from the firsthand observations made during his or her lifetime. Flies have eyes composed of thousands of lenses, but the joint action of our eyes and brain working on a text means that we can add a new facet to our worldview simply by reading a paragraph. Tapping the communal wisdom of our fellow beings is one of the tools by which we compensate for our visual limitations.

Literature can challenge our habits of seeing, expanding

our field of view, but it can also reinforce existing expectations. Validating our point of view is satisfying, but it may also carve the grooves of preference ever deeper. The suggestion that a place is "in its natural state" is usually taken to mean that visible signs of human activity—roads, buildings, quarries, fences, logging cuts—are absent. The visual-verbal distinction of "natural" versus "built" is further reinforced by media influences: calendars and television documentaries and fund-raising pamphlets from conservation organizations. As American society has grown increasingly urban and suburban—as we've transferred our homes to town and our work lives to manufacturing, office towers, and the service industry—our perception of the world around us has shifted. Just a few generations ago, home ground and workplace were often the same location. Knowledge of the local environment was a matter of life and death. Nowadays, intimacy with place tends to be avocational rather than a matter of survival: nature is increasingly synonymous with scenic.

What happens to our perception of nature, and of ourselves in nature, if our brains are in the habit of seeing as "natural" only those places where we are not?

A rhetorical question, I suppose. Except that in my explorations of my home ground I find myself fighting the impulse to crop out the human element. In the context of accounting for all the ways my vision is limited, indulging in deliberate editing seems reckless.

• • •

My point of view is confined by the orientation of my eye sockets. My body traces its solitary thread-fine path through a vast universe. Within that skinny frame of reference, my brain whittles at what's coming in with the abandon of a ruthless editor, cutting and tightening, all for my own good. What I'll be able to see of this pretty sliver of the big big world depends on how much time I'll have to spend here. So what if this amounts to decades? According to the world's clock, that span is a blip so fleeting that I can't conceive of how it might be measured.

The tyranny of the visible is that my view on the world is so ridiculously small, so limited and fragmentary, and yet what I see is so utterly central to my thought and being. My first-hand observations are immersive. They lend the authority of the eyewitness to my notions of truth and reality. Everything that's funneled into the bowl of my skull by way of my eyes and my other senses gets stirred together with everything else in there to create all that I know and feel. My awareness operates at the receiving end of the influx, giving me no choice but to be self-centered, functioning as if this perspective is all there is or all that is necessary. What emerges from the dark goo inside my head is everything that I am, all the particulars that make for personality and life experience and an idiosyncratic point of view.

Visioning seems like an intensely private act. From the smug wholeness of the perspective inside my head, it's easy to forget that everything in here—from the genetic instructions for assembling the tissues to the raw materials for the blood and the bone, from the sensation of scents and sounds and textures and flavors and images and words to the calcium that helps keep messages firing across synaptic gaps—all of it originated in the outside world.

Soon, our house will become a visible feature in that world, another element of the landscape discernible to the naked eye. Perhaps this is one of the things that provokes me into reflecting on the unseen: the house and barn and other external evidence of my existence here will be conspicuous for decades to come. For what this place has already come to mean to me, for the changes it has wrought on my psyche and in my soul—for those I have nothing outward to show.

Contemplating the Fire Seasons

By the time the calendar says winter has officially arrived, we're already deep into fire season. Each evening, a blaze in the fireplace beats back the chill brought on by days whittled short by the planet's wintry tilt. When the wind blows or the snow falls, or even on days when light clouds drift idly over, preventing the sun's warmth from streaming through the windows, I keep the fire burning all day long.

Henry David Thoreau observed that the stumps cleared from his bean patch warmed him twice—once while he was splitting them and once again as they burned in the fire, but we seem to get even more warmth from our wood. The logs we're burning now came from trees felled a few years ago, downhill from the flat area on which we've established our woodpile, which is, in turn, downhill from the house. The slope is steep, and each piece of bucked-up tree had to be hauled up to the woodpile by hand. This wasn't just a warm job, it was a downright sweaty one. After the logs spent a year or two drying, they warmed Doug as he split them, and me yet again, as I stacked the firewood and covered it for the winter. Hauling armloads of firewood up to the house accounts for a penultimate round of warming before the last, and best: the fires themselves.

I don't mind the repetitive moving of wood, since each step builds toward this toasty payoff. I love the smell of woodsmoke, and the crack and snap of kindling catching fire is a sound with deep echoes into my past. College apartments aside, it seems I've always lived in places with a fireplace or wood-burning stove. Sitting in a room transformed by soft orange light and wavering shadows is relaxing and pleasurable, and evokes a deep sense of continuity.

My contentment may also owe itself to the fact that these winter fires aren't necessary for our survival—they're cozy and help cut heating costs, but ever since we moved out of the cabin and into the house, the wood fire is not what keeps us from freezing. Still, my modern lifestyle usually keeps me well removed from the sources of food and comfort, and cliché or not, being a direct agent in meeting the fundamental need for warmth is satisfying. There's an element of ritual, of taking part in a practice that's as ancient as human culture, but there are more straightforward rewards as well. To work for an hour or two at the woodpile yields results with a bulky tangibility that my office-based work cannot match. I've seen the look, too, in my husband's eyes when two halves of a good-sized log go flying at a single stroke of the maul. He doesn't look like that when he adjusts the thermostat.

The pleasures of the winter fire season are all the more profound, too, because they stand in such sharp opposition to the uneasiness that comes with the summer fire season in our part of the western United States. Cutting and stacking require action and make me feel in control. Contrast this purposeful bustle with the grim and passive waiting that characterizes a dry summer, when the danger of forest fire soars. Some years, my nerves are set jangling in March and don't rest easy until the snow flies the following autumn. Every bit of news about scant snowpack and elusive precipitation takes on heightened significance. Daily forecasts calling for sunshine become cause for dismay. I watch afternoon thunderstorms build with a potent mixture of hope and trepidation: wishing for moisture, dreading what a lightning strike could start. Having done what we can to prepare—thinning trees, whacking down the grass and underbrush around the house, tidying up to reduce fuel for drifting embers—we can only wait.

The wood we're burning now comes from trees we cut to create defensible space—a break between the forest and our home, insurance against the rage of a forest fire. Beyond the defensible space, we continue to thin the evergreens and underbrush, extending our firebreak while ensuring a steady supply of firewood. There is an element of sacrifice to this process, but we're protecting our home, and the thinning opens the canopy to promote the health of younger trees, grasses, and wildflowers.

Our winter fires are, in the end, a peculiar merging of comforts: trees felled to bring summer peace of mind yield wood that now blazes with winter warmth. Summer's foe has switched sides, become a friend to be welcomed into the very heart of our home.

Such symmetries and equilibriums abound in the world, although I'm not always prepared to notice or acknowledge them. Similarly, I'm not always aware of the deep continuities between my daily round and the lives of my ancient forebears, not always alert to the ways in which my life directly affects my surroundings—and vice versa. To the warmth of physical work and the flare of heat in the fireplace, then, I can add this: that our wood also warms with its invitation to contemplation. I'm called to reflect on the legacies of human endeavor, on the acts of taking and giving that bind us to the world, on the beauty of trees and the loveliness of curling flames.

Weed Duty

By late spring, the season is in full swing. Weeds get an early start, even at this high elevation. As soon as their green shoots are large enough to be identifiable, I start pulling and I'll spend a few hours a week at this task right on into fall. Some of my weeding is more puttering than sustained effort, plucking a seedling here and there when I step out of the house for a few minutes or when I'm walking to or from the barn. Beyond the driveway, I make more dedicated expeditions, thinning the nearby roadsides of pennycress, pepperweed, hoary cress, thistles, sticktights, and tumbleweed.

One of the old-timers who lives nearby scoffed when I moaned about the weeds, telling me, "Mother Nature will take care of them."

I respect his judgment; his family homesteaded here in 1917, and he spent his whole life in these hills. But I pull weeds anyway. It's true that Ma Nature is good at keeping her house in order, but we humans exhibit a talent for interfering with her domestic routines, and there are a lot more of us in her abode these days. Out in these parts, people are apt to cut roads for driveways and bulldoze ground for houses and outbuildings. Every patch of disturbed earth harbors banked weed seeds, just waiting for the opportunity to sprout. We haul in gravel to maintain the roads and hay to feed our hobby livestock, and each load carries in undesirable seeds. We pretty things up with landscaping or a garden, importing exotic and occasionally aggressive plants. In this dry country, it doesn't take long for a few too many horses or llamas to overgraze a pasture, creating conditions that only a weed could love.

A weed is a plant that's not desirable in the place it's growing, so categorizing plants as weeds is a matter of context and opinion: a subjective judgment. The dandelion blooming on a lawn or golf course offends by disrupting a uniform carpet of turf. The aster in the rose garden or the grass in the perennial border or the squash plant springing up in the lettuce row violate our sense of order or composition. Human aesthetics can cut the other way with weeds, too, favoring their spread as well as their condemnation. A number of the most notorious weeds in the United States enter new habitats as ornamentals, deliberately planted and nurtured in new locations. When purple loosestrife, toadflax, dame's rocket, or bachelor's button escape the controlled habitat of the yard or garden, they can wreak ecological havoc. Free of the competitors, foragers, and pests of their homelands, such plants display an aggressive exuberance. They spread out of control, colonizing ground occupied by the native plants that sustain the local fauna or livestock grazing.

Weeds don't have to be intentionally cultivated to be a problem, of course, and crowding out forage plants is not their only offense. *Bromus tectorum*, aka cheatgrass, came to the West from the Mediterranean, most likely first arriving as packing material. In addition to a propensity for spreading quickly, it's a notorious fire hazard. Cheatgrass greens up early in the spring, absorbing water before native plants are ready to use it, then dries out quickly and catches fire easily. Surviving seeds can sprout in the ash that same year, ready to start the cycle over again the following spring. After a few repetitions of this pattern, even deep-rooted perennials may succumb to a newly established fire regime.

When nonnative plants are so badly behaved that laws are written in an effort to control them, they are labeled as "noxious." These plants earn their title both by spreading aggressively—some knapweeds emit chemicals through their roots that inhibit the growth of other plants, and leafy spurge develops tight seed capsules that pop open with enough force to eject seeds up to fifteen feet from the parent plant—and by being difficult to control. Canada thistle spreads by way of windborne seeds, but also from root nodes, each of which is capable of developing into a new plant. Tilling a stand of Canada thistle, then—or running through a roadside patch with a grader—amounts to planting a new crop.

Many plants are also considered weeds because they lack value as, or compete with, livestock forage. This criteria makes many native plants, despite their beauty or their toughness or their value as habitat or sustenance for wildlife, subject to control or extermination efforts.

I'm lucky in that the weeds around here are, for the most part, more pesky than noxious. They're still confined to small areas, particularly narrow strips along the roadways. Later in the summer I'll carry a shovel with me so I can dig out the deep-rooted perennials, but early in the summer I'm kept busy with the annuals and biennials for which pulling is an effective control. Despite the aches that creep up my back and the occasional sneezing fit brought on by dust and pollen, I prefer pulling to other control methods. This approach allows me to leave the desirable plants intact, but I'm also charmed by the simplicity of pulling: no chemicals, no tools—just me and my gloves. Early in the season, when the plants have not yet set seed, I don't even need a trash bag.

If I've fallen behind and the tumbleweeds and redroot pigweed and kochia and tumbling mustard are beginning to set seeds, I'll patrol the local roads, pulling plants and throwing them into the back of the pickup, stomping them down when the pile begins to bulge out of the bed, and pulling some more. I feel a rather unseemly joy in the way Canada thistle plants pull up after a good rain, trailing six or ten inches of pale nubby root. I'm downright smug when I see blue grama grass, alpine sage, milk-vetch, yarrow, and penstemons growing where two years ago there was a dense monocrop of pennycress.

My judgments of weediness are based more or less on a native/nonnative distinction: I pull the nonnatives and leave the rest. This system requires knowing the difference between the two, so the urge to control weeds has been instrumental to my botanical education. The endeavor has become a long-term project; there are a surprising number of plants to learn, and I often have to look them up several years in a row before the names stick in my mind. I use the term "grassland" to describe the tree-free portions of our place, but this word oversimplifies the reality. The marbled appearance of the grass-covered areas seen from a distance suggests a lack of uniformity, but the full complexity of the tapestry isn't obvious until you get closer. I once gathered some of my field guides and plopped down with them on a sunny hillside west of the house, aiming to put names to all the plants I could see and identify from where I was sitting. I hadn't yet accounted for everything as the list approached thirty names, but my brain was fed up with the effort by then and I stopped. Another day, I plucked samples of the grasses growing along the driveway to try to identify. In the space of a few minutes I collected ten different varieties.

I like feeling that my efforts to eliminate competitors for light and water will improve the chances that native plants will mature and set their own seeds. I have the satisfaction of knowing a little more about the place I've chosen to call home. I'd also like to think that I might be able to take some lessons from these well-adapted locals. With my hands occupied by the rhythms of pulling, my mind is free to ponder what these plants suggest about what it takes to fit in and survive in this environment over the long term. These plants are water thrifty. They don't crowd their neighbors. They are tolerant of hail, wind, cold, and fire.

I think my urge to pull and dig weeds comes from the sense that so many of my other activities here are a net loss for the local ecology: covering a patch of ground with a building, trapping the ground squirrels that build their nests on the engine block of the pickup, scattering a herd of elk just by walking out the door. When I'm weeding I feel like I'm contributing to the health of the landscape, giving something back.

Not everyone shares my enthusiasm for weeding, though, nor my rationale for the endeavor. I was out on the roadside a little more than a mile from the house a couple of years ago, working over some pennycress that I'd beaten back to a straggling scatter after a few summers. Natives from the grassland were spreading up onto the verge instead of the weeds creeping down into the field. Pete, one of our neighbors, rolled up next to me in his pickup on his way home. The passenger-side window slid smoothly down.

"What're you doing?!" he yelled.

"Pulling weeds," I replied.

His laugh peeled out loud and clear over the chatter of his diesel engine. I hadn't had much occasion to hang out with Pete and was impressed at the exuberance of his cackle.

"You'll never get 'em all!" he hollered cheerfully and drove away.

He was right, of course. Weeding is an errand of maintenance, not a one-time chore. I know I can't get 'em all, but
I figure that each undesirable plant I pull is a withdrawal
of a few dozen or a few hundred or, in the case of some of
the more pugnacious species, a few thousand seeds from the
soil's seed bank. I count the time spent outside—listening to
meadowlarks, awash in the smell of grass and sage, pausing
to watch a mule deer buck in velvet antlers or a mountain
bluebird hovering above the grass—as time well spent. I figure that I'll have eliminated some of the plants whose tall
stalks would have added fuel to the next grass fire that rolls
through. I figure that all Moms, whether they're keeping up
a house or a planet, appreciate a hand with the chores now
and again.

Horse Lessons

Horse crazy: as a kid, I lived the stereotype. I read all the horse books in the library, collected horse figurines, doodled horses in the margins of my school notebooks, snapped to attention whenever a horse appeared on TV or in a movie. I pranced and cantered more than I walked. Once I finally wore my parents down and got a horse, I morphed into a zealous competitor in the small pond of the local horse show scene, entering my plump buckskin mare in everything from jumping classes to gymkhana events to fifty-mile trail rides. My friends were similarly inclined, so our conversations as well as our spats revolved around horses rather than boys, clothes, or makeup. By the time I was in high school I was focused on dressage and planned to train horses for a living, but parental pressure and my mind's preference for varied input nudged me toward college. I tried boarding the sorrel gelding I was riding then, but the expense and inconvenience were too much, and I sent him back to the pasture at my dad's house.

For years, finances and circumstance made having a back-yard horse again impractical, and I pushed all things equine to my brain's back forty. After I met Doug and we moved to fourteen acres in the foothills outside of Boulder, the remuda came trotting back to the front yard. The land was steep, though, as well as rocky, heavily wooded, and lacking in grass. We could have put up a corral and sustained a horse on hay, but I had acquired a different mindset by then: wandering the slopes of Sand Gulch and Fourmile Canyon brought home the realization that I wasn't willing to sacrifice a patch of land to my equine desires. I'd begun to figure the costs of horsekeeping as something more than the price of feed and tack.

When we decided to leave Boulder, finding a place with pasture for horses was a key consideration. The hills rolling off the northern flank of Cap Rock Ridge promised to re-create my adolescent idyll of walking out of the house and going for a ride. Making the transition away from Boulder took six years, and the phased process of building stretched over another three, but in the fall of 2004, our belongings were finally in the house instead of stored in the barn, construction and landscaping projects no longer occupied all of our free time, and we had fenced a few acres adjacent to the barn. I started shopping for a horse.

This experience was like entering the seedy singles market late in life. I was old enough to know what sort of partnership I was looking for and pragmatic enough to know that I wasn't likely to find My Perfect Equine, but I wasn't quite prepared for the personal ad oversell I encountered. The "well-built athlete" showed a mean streak under saddle; the "nice mover" seemed like a dimwit; and the gelding advertised to be "about sixteen hands tall," a good size for me, turned out to be much shorter—such a dink that I didn't even bother to take my boots out of the car. Compounding the frustrations of the marketing hype was the fact that I had been, literally, out of the saddle for more than a decade. Although I took some lessons in anticipation of starting to ride again, I was awkward and out of shape. The morning after one of my first test rides, on a bay Quarter Horse gelding, I was humiliated to find bruises blooming across my seat bones.

Despite the bruised butt experience, I called the owner of the bay a few weeks later. I'd met enough rejects by then to be more appreciative of his sound limbs and mellow attitude. I packed my comfy old English saddle in the back of the car and went back for another look and a second test ride. To my fanny's relief, I found that the western saddle had been more of an issue than the horse's movement. He wasn't quite as tall as the horse of my dreams, but I liked that he was interested in what was going on around him without being flighty. He was nice looking, with all-black legs and a black mane and tail that set off his mahogany hide nicely. He came from a racing bloodline, so he had a slim build and lacked the bunchy muscling typical of his breed. White markings on his nose and forehead gave his face a friendly aspect. I negotiated terms with the owner and arranged to board Moondo (pronounced MOONdoh and named, it was said, for the Spanish word *mundo*, or "world") while I scurried around with final preparations at our place.

Blue, the red gelding I had ridden during my high school years, was in his late twenties and, like some of my old tack, had been moved around and loaned out for years but never sold. He would be coming home to live out his retirement as Moondo's companion. When the horses' homecoming day arrived, I drove out on the eastern plains to fetch Blue first. Persuaded by some grain in a bucket, he was easy to catch and followed me willingly out of his weedy pen before walking into the trailer like an old pro. Turned loose in the pasture at his new home, he trotted stiffly around for a minute looking like he could not quite believe his luck. The area was newly fenced and, other than some roaming deer and elk, had not been grazed for a decade. Blue sampled a few mouthfuls of grass, and then, in an expression of pure equine joy, lay down and rolled, flipping himself from side to side several times with shocking agility. I would have liked to have settled down to watch the old fart enjoying his new surroundings, but I had to leave to get Moondo.

By the time I arrived at his stable, the mid-November day was closing down under the weight of snow clouds. Unlike Blue, who had walked into the trailer as if he sensed I was taking him someplace more pleasant, Moondo objected to the burp in his routine. It was dinnertime. The trailer was small, dark, and unknown. I was stressed, and he knew it. He refused to load, dancing around and rearing in growing agitation. There was only one other person still at the stable, and once she finished feeding all the other horses, she helped me harass Moondo into the trailer, flicking a plastic bag tied to a whip at his heels.

I drove home on wet roads threatening to turn to ice, arriving after dark on a night without stars or a moon. I wasn't going to turn my new horse out into a pasture he'd never seen in the dark, so he didn't get the chance to explore his surroundings the way Blue had. Moondo spent his first night at his new home warm and safe, but circling unhappily in a strange stall in a strange barn, a strange horse pacing in the stall next to him. Doug and I were horse owners.

· · ·

I took my time introducing the boys to one another. Blue had been in a pen on his own for a reason when I picked him up. I'd first met him when he was three years old and knew he was submissive to the point of being clingy. His insecurity evoked contempt in other horses: they just couldn't seem to stop themselves from wanting to beat the crap out of him. For the first couple of days I kept one horse in the paddock at the barn and one in the pasture, switching them from one place to another to allow them both to graze and get acquainted with a sturdy fence between them.

I was doubtful that Moondo would turn out to be the saintly equine soul who would be tolerant of Blue. He wasn't. Once I turned them out together, Blue constantly approached Moondo, obsequiously trying to buddy up. Moondo drove him away with an escalating series of head swings, feints, and bites. Although he'd spent his entire life dodging the ire of other horses, Blue was old, stiff, and lame in the right hind leg. Scrapes and bite marks accumulated on his shaggy hide.

For the first few nights, I kept the horses shut up in their stalls to prevent nighttime altercations, but once they were both familiar with their surroundings I left the stall doors open so they could come and go as they wished. I fed them in their stalls, and Moondo soon figured out he could double-dip when it came time for evening grain. After eating his, he sauntered over to Blue's stall, pinned his ears and swung his head to send the old horse gimping out, then tucked in to a dessert of sweet and easy-to-chew senior horse chow. I was forced to insert myself in their affairs over this and began standing watch as Blue ate. Waiting at the barn was easier than closing him in and coming back later to let him out, so feeding time became a late-day interlude, a pause between working hours and whatever the evening held in store. I would check the horses over for injuries or signs of illness, would pick off ticks or spray on fly repellant in the appropriate season. Watching juncos foraging in front of the barn, enjoying part of the day's sunset episode, or listening to the rhythmic grinding of the horses' jaws as they ate were pleasant diversions from the bickering that called for my presence.

The conflicts between the horses were no surprise to me; although Blue's submissiveness was extreme, I was familiar with the dynamics of pecking among horses. My husband, though, had never been around horses before and was surprised by the differences in their personalities. Doug had imagined, I guess, a sort of generic pan-equine character type, and dominant/submissive relationship aside, Moondo and Blue could not have been more different. Blue had always been pretty obtuse, and late in life he was also partly deaf and seemed to have withdrawn into a curmudgeonly introversion. He had acquired the bad habit of walking into people as if they didn't exist. This was more obliviousness than orneriness, but it didn't make him an endearing animal to spend time with. Content with the role of retired companion horse hanging out in the pasture, he preferred to be left alone.

Moondo, by contrast, was very social toward people. If I visited him in the pasture, he would stop eating and greet me with a thorough sniffing-over. His head popped up when we came down the hill to the barn, whether on foot or driving, and he would approach the fence to assess visitors. His friendliness came with a bit of an ego, however: he expected to be admired. When it came time to offer pony rides to visiting children, Blue, as our resident plug, was pressed into grudging service, which appalled Moondo. As Blue plodded around the arena with a little kid on his back, Moondo stared in outrage, then paced, pawed, and shook his head, unable to believe that people weren't looking at, petting, or cooing over *him*.

As prey animals, horses monitor their environment pretty carefully, but Blue was apathetic as well as hard of hearing and left the task of vigilance to Moondo. This seemed to reinforce his sense of his own importance, but the extra responsibility did wear on him. In contrast to the mellowness he had exhibited before I bought him, Moondo increasingly wanted to be allowed to investigate every new item in his domain and became suspicious if anything changed: the pickup parked in a different spot, a shovel left leaning against the barn. More maddening than the skittishness itself was its intermittency. Some days he was as placid as an old milk cow; on others he seemed to be caught up in an obsessive-compulsive episode. From day to day, I never knew which horse I would have on my hands.

I'd like to say that I met the challenges of coping with his hypervigilance with the patient consistency of the horse trainer I'd once aspired to be, but Moondo's moodiness drove me nuts. Giving in to anger runs against both the noble and the practical tenets of horsemanship, which I well knew, but personality reform is not an easy task and requires practice. Minnie, the buckskin mare I had ridden as a girl, was the ideal first horse: patient with bad balance and improper riding but sly enough to instill respect. When I'd fly off the handle with her, though, she'd simply stop, anchor herself to the ground, and ignore me until I collected myself enough to ask again for what I wanted . . . nicely. Blue was less crafty, but even in his youth he had been phlegmatic and not terribly upset at my teenaged outbursts. In Moondo, I was belatedly presented with the challenge of coping with a sensitive horse. Not surprisingly, he got anxious when I got annoyed, whereupon I got more annoyed and he got more anxious. Learning to deal with my reactions to his reactions took some time, as correcting a bad habit generally does. I was also faced with unloading my preexisting ideas about how I wanted my smart horse to cope with his environment. Moondo *was* smart, but he was also a worrier, and his companions in life now were an inattentive geriatric pasture-mate and a handler who was not the calm and steady human his training had taught him to expect.

115

He was also now living in a place that posed genuine hazards. When I left the large rolling doors of the barn open one afternoon to try to flush out the fledgling Say's phoebes that had recently taken flight from their nest in the rafters, a bear got in. It pawed at (but fortunately failed to open) the metal bin where the grain was stored, spilled the jug of vinegar I had out to mix in a fly repellant preparation, left aromatic footprints up and down the breezeway, and departed. When I brought Moondo up to the barn to get ready for a ride later that day, he knew that something *bad* had been in there, and he wanted to leave. He stomped, he pawed, he shat, he snorted and fidgeted. Instead of heeding his warning and fleeing—or allowing him to do so—I left him tied to the hitching rail and persisted in walking in and out of a building that had recently housed a predator. This was the kind of cool-headed response that was supposed to give him confidence in his handler, but I suspect that this episode helped confirm Moondo's suspicions that I was a dimwit. Even old Blue, whose dimness was not in question, heeded his warnings and moved away from danger.

Had I brought Moondo home simply for his carbon-friendly off-road capabilities, or with plans to drill him in exhibition movements, our early disagreements would have led me to sell him. I had taken my time looking for an equine partner, though, because I knew I was going to be making a commitment to the horse I selected. Synchronizing needs and expectations is hard enough in human relationships, where we have the advantage of shared language. With our similar tendencies toward overreaction and taking things personally, building trust was a slow process for Moondo and me. I worked on our relationship while riding but also made time to wander out to the pasture, splitting an apple with him and Blue, scratching him to locate his itchy spots (eyebrows, base of the neck where it folds into the shoulder). I've always loved hanging out with horses, watching them eat and admiring the slick movement of muscle under polished hides, and probably it helped us both to spend time together without the pressures of trying to decipher one another's desires.

Our working relationship made a huge leap forward, too, when I got a better fix on his motivations. I was retraining him from a western way of going to dressage, which involved different applications of hands, weight, and legs. This was another source of anxiety for Moondo, but I decided to play on both his ego and his insecurity and began heaping effusive over-the-top praise on him when he gave the desired response to a cue: "Good boy! Good boy, Moondo, you are such a clever horse!" I'd pat his neck, rub his shoulder, pat his neck again, "Good boy!" This procedure made me feel silly, and it conflicted with the dignified propriety of the classical riding tradition that was my model, but there wasn't anyone around to hear my gushing, and by every inch of his bearing Moondo indicated that this was the right tool for the job. Reassured that he was on the right track, he became more willing to tune his attention on me rather than the ground squirrel scampering in front of the barn or the raven wheeling overhead. He'd always known he was clever, after all, and I suspect it was a relief to him when I began to show him that I knew it too.

I continued to pursue patience more consciously. In addition to using praise, I learned to forego riding if I was in a pissy mood. I got better at ignoring Moondo's behavior when I knew he was simply trying to keep an eye on a deer or shying at a pocket gopher next to the arena, and learned to differentiate mere distractibility from the inconsolable fits of dread that signaled something more out of the ordinary. I never succeeded in detecting what had him quivering and snorting but began to treat these episodes in the same category of experience as finding mountain lion tracks pressed in snow or freshly flipped rocks where a bear had foraged: as validation that we lived in a place where wild beings were going about the business of their lives, whether I witnessed them doing so or not.

I had entered into this chapter of horse ownership expecting to learn to be a better rider. I had been away from horses just long enough to forget that they are teachers, not just students, but on this matter, too, Moondo set me straight.

· · ·

The horses had arrived in November and spent the first winter in the small pasture adjoining the barn. The following summer, we fenced thirty-five acres on the west side of the driveway. Making peace with the line the new fence cut across a portion of my familiar view took me a while, but Moondo suffered none of my ambivalence. His range now encompassed the top of the drainage between the fingers of the west ridge, and for a horse whose self-appointed task was to keep tabs on the local goings-on, this expanded territory was paradise. He began to let his disdain for the barn pasture be known, hovering at the gate if confined there, gazing across the driveway at his precious, precious field. He also became a little territorial, hustling toward interloping deer and herding them back over the fence.

Even if Moondo seemed overly attached to his pasture, this was the manner of horsekeeping I had dreamed about for two decades. I didn't ride as often as I wanted to, but a short walk down to the barn allowed me to do so whenever I felt the urge. If I didn't have time for a ride, I could stroll out to the pasture to say hi, which was a perfect break from office work or chores around the house. We were providing the horses with water, forage, space in which to roam, and shelter (although Moondo also shunned the loafing shed we'd had built in the big pasture, sidling up to the building's exterior walls instead of going inside when he wanted to be in the shade) in a set-up that was healthier for them and less work for me than keeping them in stalls. Blue and Moondo set their own schedules, moved according to routines of their own devising, and, dinnertime aside, ate according to their preferences.

Before the horses' arrival, I tended to walk east from the house, along the crest of the ridge, making my way back home along the game trails crisscrossing the wooded side-hill. I now had an incentive to consider the horses' relationships to their home ground. The bowl's slope captured the morning rays, and the boys soon picked out favorite spots for napping; trailing them there, I learned that these were places where the wind eddied to calm. With his shambling gait, Blue was not fond of the rockier areas around the perimeter of the bowl and spent most of his time low in the basin where the footing was more even and most of the grass was fine-textured blue grama. Moondo seemed to enjoy variety in his grazing, giving a clump of mountain muhly a flat-top trim with a single bite and then seasoning the mouthful with a frond of yarrow. When he came across them, he devoured dandelions, showing a taste for bitter greens. If the grass was going to seed, he twirled the heads together with his upper lip and yanked them out, leaving the leafy blades for another day. He was fond of the fuzzy white flowers of Platte thistles, plants so spiniferous that I don't dare touch them without gloves on. After carefully nipping a bulbous blossom off, he would take his time rolling the morsel around in his mouth to position it for chewing with a minimum of poking.

Watching the horses was easier than watching wild animals, who tend to flee when they detect my presence. I could ogle the horses as long as I wished, without trying to be sneaky and without relying on the house as a wildlife blind.

I also had the luxury of knowing I was seeing the same individuals on a regular basis. With a few exceptions—the raven with the crippled foot, the doe with a long split cleaving her left ear—wild animals are anonymous, indistinguishable from one another. I can say that Moondo and Blue had preferences and personality traits because I knew I was seeing the same animals from day to day and month to month.

My ventures out to the pasture were social visits, but they were conducted in the same spirit as my nature walks. The intent was to break free of the interiority of both the walls of the house and the confines of my cerebral preoccupations. I watched the horses in much the same way as I watched birds and ungulates: as an opportunity to spy on independent lives unfolding according to the manner of their species. The relative liberty of their pasture life freed the horses from the confinement and regimented routine of life at a stable and gave them space to exercise their preferences and express their personalities.

In capsule form, the process of domestication goes something like this: humans in the ancient world captured certain wild animals and tamed them. Some species, notably dogs and horses, demonstrated both a talent for learning commands and the ability to perform useful tasks, so people began to train and breed them for specialized jobs. They bred more of the animals that were docile and trainable and either ate or bred fewer of the ones that were mean, rambunctious, or obstinate. Human selective pressures thus created a new category of animal, defined in large part by the fact that they're adapted to live under human care and control.

This story can be interpreted as a chronicle of diminishment, in which wiliness and self-reliance are eroded to servility and meekness, but I think this misrepresents the reality. Domestication gave animals the luxury of protection and released them from the imperative for vigilance as a matter of survival, but it also demanded the expression of other abilities. Evolution isn't generally erosional. The adaptations that enabled domestic animals to find a fit with their human-managed environment did not replace the inborn traits of their species.

The relationships they pursue with other horses may be truncated by stall panels and fences, but horses create bonds and live by ancient equine customs, conducted by way of a gestural language that's universal among their kind. The most lasting training methods used with horses build on their inherent behaviors and make use of equine social patterns—qualities that were neither implanted by selective breeding nor eliminated by it. Moondo's responses to the untamed aspects of his surroundings showed that he retained plenty of the keenness of a wild critter. I was motivated to continue the ritual of feeding time in part because I didn't want Moondo to be thinking that his field provided *everything* he needed for a contented life.

• • •

A year and a half after we brought the horses to their new home, it became clear that it was time to let Blue go. He fell one day while I was out of town, and it took both Doug and a veterinarian to get the old horse back on his feet. By the time I got home a few days later, Blue had already fallen again at least once; Doug was able to get him up, but his stability was gone. His hindquarters would teeter farther and farther over until he had to throw his weak hind leg out to catch himself, winding up faced ninety degrees from where he'd been. This curlicue locomotion was treacherous and tiring. He could no longer stand with one hind leg cocked in a resting posture, and he had become afraid to lie down, knowing he might not be able to get up again.

He was clearly exhausted, and we began making arrangements to have him put down. Given the choice, I wanted Blue to die in circumstances of relative peace, before he got hurt in a fall, at a time when both Doug and I could be present, in a place where it would be easy to deal with his remains.

I solicited advice from a couple of veterinarians on what to do with Moondo when we had Blue euthanized. The old-school guy told me I should give Moondo a sedative and isolate him from the event. Our new vet, the young woman who had come out to help Doug the first time Blue fell, advised us to not let him observe the euthanasia but to allow him to see and sniff the body afterward. When she arrived on the appointed day, I put Moondo's halter on him and took him for a walk down the driveway while Doug held Blue. We hadn't gone far before the vet drove past us on her way out. She gave a short wave, but didn't stop.

I turned Moondo around and we headed back to the barn. Once we topped the slight rise at the end of the driveway, I could see Blue, lying on his side in the parking area in front of the barn. When Moondo noticed him, his ears pricked up and he stared intently and began testing the air with deep breaths. By the time we were a hundred yards away, he was rigid, head high and nostrils wide in the familiar posture telegraphing that something was terribly wrong and that we should get out of here *now*. He slowed, snorting and staring, then stopped a few yards away from the body, refusing to move closer. Holding the end of the lead rope, I walked to Blue's head and bent down to pat him one last time.

The moment I touched Blue's unresponsive forehead, Moondo's head dropped and his body sagged, the alarm draining out of him. I don't know how horses process the concept of death, but I no longer have any doubt that they do. Moondo understood that Blue was dead. He stepped forward and sniffed the old horse's nose, and stood for a few minutes, head down. When he listlessly picked at a patch of nearby grass, I guessed that he had investigated enough and turned him loose in the barn pasture. Instead of heading toward the gate leading to his favorite field, Moondo stood quietly near the barn, looking at Blue's body.

Moondo and Blue had not exactly been best friends, but they had been their own little herd, and I braced myself for the separation anxiety I expected once Blue was hauled away. Instead of pacing and running around the pasture whinnying, however, Moondo persisted with the stoic demeanor he'd shown after he had determined that Blue was dead. He called out a couple of times when I took him on trail rides over the next few weeks, but those vocalizations had an aspect of a query rather than desperation or distress. He seemed to understand that Blue was gone and not merely displaced.

None of which is to say that the event didn't affect him. He was depressed, refusing to come in from the big pasture for grain several nights. He began napping with his nose nearly touching a boulder that jutted from the ground out in the basin, an eminence we dubbed Companion Rock. His beloved field seemed to offer solace during his period of mourning. We made a point of visiting him several times a day, and he expressed his appreciation by grooming our necks and shoulders with his lip as we patted him.

• • •

I began horse shopping again, this time looking for a mount that would be suitable for Doug. Perhaps because he would have the final say, this search was less fraught for me, although it did entail hours of sifting through ads and making phone calls, lots of driving, and a couple of hair-raising trial rides. About five weeks into the search, we were at a stable with several Tennessee Walking horses for sale. Out on the trail, Doug asked the wrangler whether he could let Max, the tall black gelding he was trying out, go into his fast gait. When they took off together, I could sense Doug's grin by his posture in the saddle and knew we had found his horse.

Had Moondo been given a say in the selection process, I'm sure he would have requested a companion who would honor his position as obvious and deserving sovereign. Unfortunately for Moondo, Max was both big and dominant. I again took the precaution of keeping the horses separated for several days, letting them meet first on opposite sides of the pipe corral fence, but scrapping was inevitable when I turned them loose together. Max, it seemed, had spent much of his life living in confined areas with lots of other horses, and he was accustomed to getting his way with the aid of excellent timing, good aim, and conviction. Max didn't threaten to bite or kick, he bit or kicked. Unlike Blue, who had approached other horses timidly, hoping to make friends, Moondo set the tone by trying to boss Max around. This didn't go over well, and under the new order I saw Moondo's haughtiness in a new light. In the larger equine scheme of things, he wasn't a dominant horse after all, and the fact that he'd been the lead horse during his time with Blue had gone to his head. Moondo soon accumulated more scrapes and bald patches than Blue ever had. Grooming him in preparation for riding one day, I found a swelling on his haunch in the perfect form of a hoof print.

In contrast to his aggressiveness toward Moondo, Max was polite in his dealings with Doug and me. He tested the house rules and, once corrected, seemed satisfied to know what his boundaries were. He was afraid of whips, and I suspected that his good manners were also a way of minimizing conflicts with people. Unhappy events in his past may have contributed to his aloofness, although his reticence toward people was different from that of old Blue. Max acknowledged us as a part of his world, but seemed to regard the relationship as a professional rather than a social one. He enjoyed getting out on the trail with Doug, but seemed confused when we paid a visit in the pasture. He accepted attention, but didn't seek it out. He was with us almost a year before he could bring himself to yield to the pleasure of a good scratch between the ears, his eyelids and lower lip drooping in surrender, and even then his expression afterward suggested he felt a little dirty about it.

His dignified demeanor was somewhat undermined by a gangly appearance: his ears were long, his head was big, his back was slightly swayed, and his front feet splayed out. Like Moondo, Max was observant of his environment, but he directed his attention differently, checking gate latches as he was passing them and watching closely if anyone was around the barn, where he knew the grain was stored. He demonstrated his understanding of quick-release knots by untying himself and his civility by continuing to stand where he'd been left after he'd done so.

Max liked the pasture fine, but he also loved the barn: if left on his own while I rode Moondo out on the trail, he retreated there to await our return. He enjoyed partaking of its shade in summer and protection from the wind in winter, despite growing a winter coat that would put a wooly mammoth to shame. Moondo persisted in despising the barn and protested the changeover to the winter routine of spending nights in the small pasture attached to it by trying to evade being herded through the gate. Once locked in, he would eat his grain and then hurry back out to verify that he really was incarcerated. When Doug walked down to feed and let the horses out to the big pasture on snowy mornings, Max was usually standing either in the doorway of his stall or under the shed roof of the barn, dry and comfy-looking, while

Moondo, covered in snow with icicles jingling in his tail, stomped impatiently by the gate.

I had hoped to be able to abandon the practice of standing guard during feeding time, but I merely switched my role from shooing Moondo to shooing Max. Gulping food was a habit he had acquired from living in a paddock with other horses, and Max could vacuum up his grain before Moondo, with his preference for chewing reflectively while surveying his domain, was halfway finished. If they were eating in the barn in the winter, Max liked to bang the divider between the stalls with his forefoot, sending Moondo shooting outside to investigate the danger, dinner forgotten.

To say that Max was polite is not to say he always agreed with us, although he was ingenious in expressing his opposition. The horses went barefoot, but Max was ouchy when we rode on the gravel roads, so we got him hoof boots. He hated them, no doubt in part because we laughed at him the first time we put them on. We couldn't help ourselves; he had big feet to begin with, and with the rubber cups clamped on them he looked like a little kid wearing his dad's shoes. Ordinarily exuberant out on the trail, he scuffed down the road exhibiting the most successful sulky expression I've ever seen on a horse.

Getting ready for a ride one day after we had used the boots a few times, I had Max's forefoot between my knees and was trying to wrestle a boot onto his hoof when his leg gave way. I jumped back, and we spent a few anxious minutes checking him over. We couldn't find anything wrong, so I picked up his foot and was starting to reposition the boot when his forelegs buckled and he dropped to his knees again. When I stepped aside this time, he promptly stood back up, regarding me blandly. Instead of throwing a fit, he opted to lie down in nonviolent protest. He won that argument, and we shelved the boots.

There was little question that Max was the bigger, stronger, more dominant horse, but Moondo, undaunted by Max's assertiveness, was uppity and persistent. After a time, they developed something of a power-sharing agreement and settled into a mostly agreeable companionship. Moondo showed Max where the good sunning spots were and taught him how to eat Platte thistle flowers. Moondo was allowed to assume the lead position when coming in for dinner and setting the schedule for the day's wandering in the pasture. Out riding, Max led, period. Moondo's lesser standing was also evident in the fact that if Max so much as twitched his ears toward a threatening position, Moondo scooted away, whereas Max ignored Moondo's full repertoire of threat postures, from head swinging to ear pinning to half-kicking hind legs. Max was similarly unimpressed by pointless acts of bravado, such as Moondo's snatching a mouthful of hay from the pile assigned to Max before scampering over to his own.

By and large, though, I think Moondo was more content. He wasn't Lead Horse, but he also wasn't the only one on the place keeping an eye on things. They took turns at nap time, one horse conking out on his side while the other dozed standing up, on half-alert. And to his delight, Moondo was put in charge of providing kiddy rides. Blue may have been slow-moving, but he was unmindful of people and we always had to make sure he didn't knock anyone down. Moondo, in contrast, was captivated by small humans and moved very carefully around them. He thrilled visiting kids with careful head-to-toe sniffed greetings and nibbled the treats they offered more delicately than the spiniest Platte thistle flower. With a child on his back, his walk slowed to a deliberate pace that he never used with me.

• • •

Max had arrived in August, toward the end of the summer monsoon season, and we found out pretty quickly that trees were his preferred shelter from rain. This is a bad strategy in our lightning-prone environment, and Moondo knew it. When distant rumbling signaled that a thunderstorm was on its way, he would go after Max like a crazed cutting horse, lunging and feinting with pinned ears and bared teeth, trying to drive him toward the low-lying bowl in the big pasture. Max ignored him.

The following summer, I fenced off the section of pasture with the trees on it. The summer after that, I was prepared to take the same precaution again, but something had changed in Max. Once again, when thunder began growling, he would head for one of the trees, but when Moondo began harassing him, he relented and followed Moondo's lead out to the bowl of the pasture. Before long, they both headed for low ground at the first signs of an approaching storm.

I wonder what nuance in their relationship allowed Moondo to persuade Max that he shouldn't stand under a tree in a thunderstorm. And, more interestingly, where did Moondo learn this? He didn't come by the knowledge as a result of training. His impulse to flee high ground is an item of cultural knowledge, a nugget of wisdom passed on to him at the side of his dam, or, possibly, learned from firsthand observation. Despite the many ways that humanity has shaped horses through the process of domestication, and despite the ways we exert control over their existence day by day, the knowledge they have is not limited to what people have taught them. Max's change of heart regarding the proper behavior in the face of a thunderstorm shows that descriptions of equine social behavior that fall back on the simple terms of dominance and submission are caricatures: they emphasize certain characteristics while leaving much out. Pecking orders exist, and they do matter, but horses, like people, respond to the particulars of a situation, an environment, their companions, and combinations thereof.

What researchers know about equine cognition indicates that horses lack higher executive functions, such as the capacity for abstract thought or the ability to imagine the future. Horses may know what death is when they see it, but they don't fret about their own mortality. Memory is a different matter. They almost certainly don't store detailed recollections the way people do, but anyone who has rehabilitated an abused horse or tried to overcome a simple training error knows that horses readily make associations between past experience and present circumstances. I doubt Max suffers flashbacks about being beaten, but the quality of his attention when a whip or walking stick is evident shows that long items in peoples' hands are significant to him. He doesn't worry about where the stick or whip is when he can't see it, however: out of sight, out of mind.

A good portion of the big pasture is visible from my west-facing office window, and I seldom stand up from my desk without looking out to see whether the horses are in sight. If they are, I'll often spy on them through binoculars. Usually, they're grazing at a leisurely pace, walking step by step on a course that wanders from one vegetative tidbit to the next. I love it when I look out and they're lying down. The comparative rarity of the position grabs my attention; seeing them napping with legs bundled next to their bellies, noses almost touching the ground, reassures me that all is well: they are well-fed, comfortable, at ease, content. At the same time, my throat tightens. They look so small out on that big grassy expanse.

Every once in a while, I'll catch them playing with one another: mock-fighting by nipping at the other's face, neck, and forelegs, then breaking away for a quick round of chase complete with bucks and high-flying kicks. This is something I never see when I'm out walking in the pasture—they simply don't engage in this behavior when I'm around. If I walk into sight or drive in along the road when they're playing, they'll abruptly stop and look at me. I think it's just that their attention has been diverted away from their game, but it looks like they're trying to avoid being watched—as if they want to shield this aspect of their lives from my prying eyes.

Our move to Cap Rock, with its grass-clothed expanses, was inspired by the desire to have horses in our lives. The presence of Moondo and Blue and Max expanded the way I interact with the landscape around me. Through them I have been urged toward a regard for and appreciation of the land that requires attention to more than just the prettiness of the view. The land sustains my psyche, but it sustains the horses' lives in a more fundamental way. The responsibility to keep them well and happy has to be balanced against an obligation to keep the grasslands from getting overgrazed or overrun by weeds. The need to contain the horses calls for fencing that also allows deer and elk to pass through as easily and safely as possible. I observe the horses much as I watch the land: to better acquaint myself with an aspect of the world that is not connected to an electric switch, to learn things I don't know, to discover questions I haven't thought to ask before.

Out walking, I'll often whistle or holler at the boys until they look up at me, then wave to them. Driving past the pasture on the way to town to run errands, I'll toot the horn. I call their attention because it amuses me, but also because I like to remind them that I'm part of their world, even when I'm not in their physical presence—much as they're often on my mind, even when I'm not with them.

Picking Up the Unexpected

The excavation of our house site a few years ago left an angled bank of bare dirt on the east side. Below this, broken rocks had rolled and lay scattered among the native bunch-grass. The pink knobs of granite looked messy in the greenery, and I knew that any time I walked along the hill on that side of the house I'd be risking my ankles on the loose stones.

So I began gathering the rocks and stacking them along the base of the bare dirt, creating a foundation to hold the soil against our pounding summer thunderstorms. The dirt that didn't get covered with the dry-stacked rocks would be planted with wildflower seed, and in a year or two the ugly barren slope would begin to blend with its surroundings.

Given the roughness of the terrain, a wheelbarrow was out of the question; I had to carry each rock up the hill before placing it on the slope. I started with the big ones, rolling those nearest the base of the dirt into place with grunts and stinging forearms, then staggering up the hill with the lunkers that had rolled farther out cradled in my arms. With all the puffing and groaning, I seldom worked on this chore when anyone else was around.

With a ribbon of large stones strung along the bottom of the slope, I started in on slightly smaller rocks, lugging them up and dropping them with a thud, one by one. I eventually worked my way down to those I could carry two or three at a time, and then finally started collecting the smallest, the ankle-busters the size of tennis balls and plums. These chinked the gaps between rocks I'd already placed, locking all the pieces together. It was boring work, but also soothing in a way. The pacing rhythm, walking up and down the hill, working my way side to side along the slope, was oddly meditative.

The monotony of pick, plod, plop; pick, plod, plop was broken now and again when I picked up a rock that had formed the roof of an anthill, or sent a spider scuttling, or exposed a black stinkbug that promptly began waving its fanny in the air. Some of the rocks had spider egg cases—cottony white and shaped like a lentil—glued to the bottom. Focused on my mission of gathering the loose rocks and stabilizing the slope, I used these stones anyway, though I set them down carefully, trying to position them so that the arachnid nurseries were sheltered and wouldn't be crushed.

One day, I picked up a stone the size of an open hand. I noticed, and ignored, an egg case on the bottom—until I turned the rock over again before setting it down. There was the egg case, but straddling it, in an unmistakably protective posture, was a spider.

I hadn't seen her when I grabbed the rock, and she didn't scurry up my arm or make a leap for freedom as I walked up the hill. Instead, she planted herself over the eggs, each of her eight legs sprawled to grip the edges of the lens-shaped casing. The soft tan of the spider's slim body, neatly striped with black lines, stood out sharply against the snowy background.

I stared for a moment and—slowly, carefully—set the rock down so that the spider, still clutching the white disc of eggs, was in a nook, out of sight and out of the sun.

I usually found it hard to call a halt to my rock-stacking chore; I would inevitably pass a rock on the way to the house and think, *Ah, I know just where to put that one.* Instead of stopping, I would return for that particular stone, whereupon the same thing would happen again, and then again. On that day, though, when I set the rock and its occupants down, I walked away. The creature's boldness in the face of a threat so much larger than herself had upset my rhythm.

Perhaps I was struck by the juxtaposition; many of us tend to think of spiders as ominous or creepy, a reputation that clashes with that beautiful image of protectiveness. But what has really stuck with me is the sense of quiet determination I glimpsed that day. Maybe it's silly to make so much of what is, when you think about it, a pretty ordinary event. Yet the spider's behavior suggested bigger things. It suggested the possibilities of individual determination, and it was a reminder that aggression and retreat are not the only options in the face of trouble. I walked away with the vivid image of that slender body thrown between the giant that was me and the small cluster of eggs, a portrait in my mind of the potency of the simple act of standing up for what matters.

Winter Outlook

Soon after the grass greens up in late spring, it will tan to a persistent tawny hue. I admire how it ripples like fur in the afternoons of late summer, but its arrangement over the terrain and among rocks, shrubs, and trees settles into a familiar routine for my eyes. Even when bursts of sulfur yellow, orange, and maroon break out among the gambel oak and aspens for a few weeks in the fall, the organizing theme of flora and earth remains the same.

I appreciate our surroundings whatever the season, but it turns out that my eyes are less likely to be lulled into complacency during the winter months. Fall snowstorms are often followed by an interlude of Indian Summer when the sky gleams like unveined turquoise. A fast-moving squall might bring whiteout conditions that are followed a half hour later by full sunshine. An unsettled atmosphere sends clouds roaming past one another, moving in different directions at different altitudes. The days are framed by long sunrises and sunsets that can wrap the horizon full circle with pastel bands of peach, lilac, and gunmetal gray. The night sky presents itself early each evening, and the cold air lends the stars extra glint, the Milky Way's ribbon extra glow. Fog, hoarfrost, sunshine, wild temperature swings, cloud ceilings low and high, wind and calm: the view varies greatly day by day, even hour by hour.

Our winters are not the simple buildup of powder you might expect in a place with an elevation higher than the base of many ski areas. The transformation of the land by a veneer of white is usually fleeting. On south-facing slopes, rocks and grass tufts poking through the snow cover create islets of warmth. These dark freckles grow and merge until the vista has resumed its fawn coloration. If the snowfall is light, this metamorphosis takes place in a matter of hours. If the new snow is deep, it will take a few sunny days. And because this happens so much faster on south-facing slopes, there is a time after each storm when the surrounding hills are two-faced: grassy on their south- and west-facing slopes, snow-covered on the east and north. We frequently have open winters, in which snowy enrobement and sunny erasure create shifting skewbald patterns across the landscape from the first snow to the last.

On an autumn night, I might go to bed listening to the faint ticking of raindrops on the roof, awake to silence, and think the precipitation has stopped. Instead, I'll look out the window and find my world remade. I feel as if I've been given the gift of clean, with dusty ground and weathered grass tucked under a smooth coverlet of white. Gardening projects that didn't get finished, scattered rocks from a landscaping project, a jumble of firewood not yet stacked and covered are all transformed into generic humps. The rigid structures and hard emblems of modernity—cars, buildings, fences, walls—are hidden. The land's familiar contours are still there, but they're rounded and plumped, the angles softened. The enfolding quiet is like a summons to reflection and solitude. In late evening I'll sometimes bundle up and go outside to fall backwards into a pillowy bed of snow to look at the stars and listen to the near-perfect stillness. As often as I've seen the transformation, the serenity and flowing concealment of new-fallen snow still charm me. Sitting down at the window with a cup of tea is a deep pleasure, one of those moments when I simultaneously feel basic needs—for warmth and sustenance—and find them met.

A covering snowfall evokes freshness, but the canvas doesn't stay blank for long. I know the animals are here all year long, but the signs they leave are hard for me to read in tall grass or hard-packed dirt. After a snow that has smoothed the topography, I enjoy taking unhurried strolls to see who's been out, and where. I might discover that a rabbit sheltered in the buried end of the gutter downspout by following the chain of Y-shaped links dimpled into the snow: two parallel tracks for the long hind feet, the forefeet so close together that they leave a one dip with two offset lobes. The deer leave trails like stitching, the dragging of their hooves the thread between the tacked-down prints.

Oval divots show the press of coyotes' feet. Up here in ranching territory, the coyotes prefer to be heard and not seen, but they like to travel along the local roads. After a snow, a line of tracks will stipple the unplowed ribbon with faint gray type. The script veers to the margin of the ditch now and again, where a snuffled hole will reveal the entry to a rodent tunnel. Those tunnels are invisible when the snow is deep enough, but the burrowers sometimes periscope to the surface, leaving an isolated hole that gives away their subsurface activity. If the snowfall is scant, the rodents must travel like the rest of us, on top of the snow. I once followed the trail of a mouse from the barn, where it presumably spent the night foraging for dropped grain and seeds from the horses' hay. The tracks, unwavering, followed the edge of the driveway and continued along the gravel road until they made a sharp turn and disappeared under a clump of fescue. Later, I used the car's odometer to check the distance: a little over a tenth of a mile.

The verges of the roads, where the seeds of lamb's quarters and other weedy plants accumulate and the thatch of grass is kept at bay by grading and plowing, are also popular with the juncos. The birds' feet leave wiry marks that paint the snow's canvas with cuneiform impressions, converging here and there into brown scribbles where the birds scratched down to dirt in their search for seeds.

Occasionally, the wind will kick up just after snow has fallen, scrubbing away the loose accumulations but leaving daubs wherever it was compacted. On the uniform brown of the gravel road, I can see the white boot prints from Doug's morning walk a half mile away. The path of a coyote trotting purposefully along is rendered like a short Braille phrase repeated over and over. The paired white lines left by a car's passage offer a clean abstract image that manages to suggest lonely passage.

Down on the north-facing slopes, snow gussies up the pine and spruce, calling to mind crowds of girls in puffy party dresses. The white poufs and mounds are a festive change from the trees' usual evergreen attire. More distant groves, which normally appear as inky blotches, are, for a time, speckled gray and soft. Clark's nutcrackers flock to the treetops, yakking at one another and glittering the air with small flurries loosed from the branches.

Compared with the intricate marks the animals leave, the path of my own feet, swollen by warm winter boots, seems awkward and clumsy. The rabbit's prints, the trail of the coyote, the juncos' scuffles—all seem to be guided by purpose and need, while the shuffled evidence of my own passing suggests indecision or the wavering of the lost. In reality, though, the meanders in my path merely indicate where my attention has been pulled away from the task of walking as I track the new season.

None of which is to say that winter is universally charming, particularly given that winter weather can arrive with all seriousness any time from September to May. By December 21, the traditional first day of winter, we've been through weeks of cold and, unless it's been a drought year, multiple storms. As the first day of winter, the date is meaningless, but as the solstice, signaling the onset of incrementally longer days, I find it more significant with each passing year. I appreciate the extra minutes of daylight as compensation for the arrival of blizzard season. Once the new year ticks over, the weather rarely offers those storybook snows of gracefully toppling flakes accumulating in a uniform blanket. Instead, I'll look out the kitchen window and note that the snow is whizzing past the evergreen backdrop with a distinct uphill slant, as the wind drives it over the flank of the ridge. Instead of enveloping silence, we crawl into bed with the house moaning and shuddering in a shoving match with the wind that might last for days.

Other than two years I lived in England during college, I've spent every winter of my life in Colorado, and I thought I had a pretty good handle on what the season can be like. When we moved up here, though, I discovered that Colorado winters still have plenty to teach me. In my life before moving to Cap Rock, for example, snow was a substance that needed to be rolled or otherwise compacted to make a throwable ball or a snowman. Now I know that a synergy of wind and snow can weld the latter into a substance with considerable structural integrity.

We call the super-hardened stuff that accumulates during a particularly bad drifting event "snowment" (persnickety readers may protest that "snowcrete" is the more technically correct term, but I suspect even the most strict of them will agree that under the rules of both punning and poetic license, "snowment" has a better ring). Snowment differs from merely crusty snow in that it's not only hard enough for a person to walk on, it's hard enough to support a horse, each hoof barely leaving a crease. We once had a storm leave snowment drifts about two feet deep along a seventy-foot stretch of the driveway. We started using a pickaxe to break them up, but when it became clear that the process was going to take days, we waited till the next morning and, when the snow was at its hardest, drove our cars out over the top. You could barely see the tracks.

Shoveling snowment in the conventional manner is impossible: even if you're able to lever the edge of a shovel in, the drift is fused into a single structure that weighs hundreds of pounds. Breaking such snow from the bottom up is debilitating; our preferred method now is to plunge a garden spade in from the top and lever off chunks to be pitched away by hand. This activity explains why I'll emerge from a snowy winter more fit than when I went in.

Snowment is so hard that even using the snowplow is a challenge: the blade has a tendency to ski up the surface of the drift instead of biting in. We've learned from unhappy experience to be alert for this phenomenon, because if you're not paying attention the truck will follow the plow up onto the drift, and we have yet to encounter a drift hard enough to support the combined weight of the truck and plow. If the drift is deep enough, when the wheels punch through the weight of the vehicle's undercarriage will be nicely distributed across a solid platform that must be disassembled piece by piece before the tires can find their grip. Digging hard-packed snow out from under a truck while lying on your side or belly is hard work, and any sense of victory at being able to drive the vehicle out is overridden not only by the knowledge that you got yourself into the predicament in the first place, but also by the realization that you're already pooped and the task of snow-clearing still remains.

The challenges of drifting snow are compounded by the fact that drifting can occur regardless of whether snow is falling or not. In fact, the worst drifts occur when the sun is out to melt the snow and fuse the icy grains together more effectively. One sunny Valentine's Day, Doug and I went to town for a date night, and arrived home about noon the next day. The sun was cheerfully shining and the roads were clear and dry—except for a seventy-yard section where the snow was packed onto the roadway to a depth of about four feet. We walked the last half-mile home, lugging our groceries, and called some neighbors to beg their help. I don't remember which one of us was driving when we arrived back at the blocked section of road with the truck and plow, but I do recall that after the truck high-centered in the afore-described fashion, I was the one who dug it out. The others were working plenty hard, though, chunking up the drift. After about six hours, we had a path just wide enough for a car, with walls higher than the vehicle's roof. That was the first day we mulled buying shares in a backhoe, but it wasn't the last. Our low-budget solution has been to park strategically when conditions indicate a drift event is in the making, leaving a car out on the road beyond the most likely drift points.

Although I don't like having to go outside when the wind is constructing the drifts, I do like to wander around after the shoveling is done and the atmosphere has calmed down. I admire the riffles and purls and frozen standing waves: captive fluidity in this arid land. This is the deepest charm of winter, I suppose: with the precipitation arriving in frozen form, evaporation is stalled. We enjoy the suggestion of wetness more enduringly than in summer, when the rain arrives with a flash and a crash and rushes away downhill or soaks quickly into the thirsty soil. On some winter days, we're in the clouds rather than below them. Vapor shrouds the buttes and curls among the trees, the mist veiling all that is bristly and rough. Dampness darkens the trunks of trees and sets fractal rosettes of lichen off from their background of stone with sharp contrast. On days when fog creeps up from the Arkansas River Valley, it fills drainages and low-lying basins like a milky sea. Buttes rise from the froth like islands, and for a few hours the view is more coastal than rocky mountain high. Such misty days offer not only the idea of wetness, but the real thing: in the dead of winter, the air smells of rain.

Groundhog Day, like the first day of winter, is irrelevant as a marker of the season's change—winter, in my experience, has *never* ended in early February. Like the winter solstice, however, the date ratchets up in my awareness as the years pass. I acknowledge it as a plausible hump day, when the winter has crested and entered its uneven course toward spring.

Our last frost date is usually around Memorial Day, so this is a lengthy ride. By early April, I'm itching to move the heavy coat and boots to the back of the closet. I finger my short-sleeved shirts wistfully: summer, with all its scenic predictability, is awfully appealing. I begin to think what a nice switch it will be to walk on ground that's not slicked with snow and ice. I imagine sitting on the deck in the evening, watching shadows stretch across the land's pale green pelt. I picture dark-bellied clouds coalescing into a thunderhead, casting tree-flecked meadows into shade, testing the ground with white-hot forks of lightning.

Fourmile Postscript

On Labor Day 2010, my former home ground west of Boulder gained national attention when a fierce wind-driven fire began to rip through steep canyons and dense ponderosa forest in what has since become known as the Fourmile Canyon Fire. The day after the fire started, Doug called Stephanie, one of our former neighbors. She, her husband, and their two teenaged sons had evacuated in a frenzy, grabbing too many of the wrong things, and then driven to a vantage point on Flagstaff Mountain, south of the fire zone. They arrived in time to watch their house explode in the flames.

That evening, I talked to Marcy, another of our old neighbors. Like us, she had moved away from Fourmile Canyon a few years before the fire and was watching the events unfold from a distance. "It's the disaster we all tried to prepare ourselves for," she said.

Yes, I thought, it sure is—even though I was safely removed from the fire, more than a hundred miles from the people dealing with chaos and loss. I wasn't going to be looking for a new place to live, trying to settle kids in school clad in second-hand shirts, inventorying losses for insurance, deciding whether to rebuild, finding a way to do so. Instead, I became hyperaware of the intact minutiae of our house, such as the grouping of family photos I'd finally gotten around to framing and arranging in the hall. Books shelved in my office, some signed by their authors; jewelry my husband made for me; the elk-tooth pendant my dad gave me decades ago; the wooden horse my mother's Uncle Joe carved: I tried to refresh my appreciation for these objects, then willed myself to make peace with their impermanence. Outside, ponderosas sketched their familiar bristly forms against a backdrop of fall grasses, baked by the sun of a dry summer to shades of biscuit and toast, bouncing rhythmically in the autumn wind.

I don't usually fritter away chunks of time on the Internet, but in the days after the fire I searched for everything I could find about it. Marcy had emailed me a link to a satellite image website and I zoomed in to look for our former home. The color-infrared image rendered intact vegetation in red, and there, adjacent to a 180-degree loop thrown by Fourmile Canyon Drive, I could see the outline of the roof among rust-colored splotches. Our old house had survived. The distance between it and the stark gray foundations of incinerated houses was breathtakingly short.

The reports I read didn't offer much I didn't already know in terms of fire risk. I was aware that the forests outside of Boulder were thick and overgrown, that the terrain was steep, that the roads were narrow and winding, that the region was suffering under drought conditions. I already knew that the canyons were densely populated, although I did learn from a report issued by Headwaters Economics that Boulder County ranked first in Colorado and number ten among all the counties in eleven western states for its density of housing in wooded areas.

The Fourmile fire was, in a sense, a perfect firestorm. Seventy-mile-per-hour winds started whipping across those densely built foothills at the tail end of an extremely dry summer. The gusts found embers lingering from a stack of slash that had been burned and doused on a calm day the week before; once alight, the fire spread rapidly. Dispatch and 911 call reports indicate that wind-lofted firebrands were igniting spot fires fewer than twenty-five minutes after the fire was initially reported. In its run of just three days, the fire burned about six thousand acres and destroyed 168 structures, making it, at the time, the costliest wildfire in state history.

I was riding a strange emotional pendulum. Anxious and spooked one minute, I would veer toward shame the next, feeling self-indulgent for claiming any part of what was not my disaster. I felt prudently cautious for trying to learn more about the fire's dynamics, then accused myself of being a voyeur. We had left Fourmile Canyon nine years before. The tree cover here in central Colorado is not as dense as it was on our property in Fourmile Canyon, and the evergreen stands are broken up by grasslands. But our summer had also been frightfully dry, and our autumn was getting windy. Fremont County imposed a fire ban, which our newest neighbors, who were fond of burning in their outdoor fire pit, dismissed as government interference. I acquired the habit of looking out the west-facing windows, watching for smoke coming from the ridge where their new house was emerging from the trees.

. . .

Every region of the country has at least one iconic natural disaster or weather-related hazard associated with its location: hurricanes and tsunamis on the coasts; earthquakes and volcanic eruptions in fault zones; tornadoes, blizzards, ice storms, and floods on the plains; storms, landslides, and avalanches in the mountains. Life on a dynamic and beautiful planet offers no exemption from disaster, no freedom from uncertainty, no release from risks that are catastrophic on a human scale, however run-of-the-mill they may be in geologic terms. No one place is assuredly safe.

Wildfire is the disaster most characteristic of where I live, so it isn't surprising that I'm sensitive to it. Beyond this firsthand connection, though, I'm convinced that the American attitude toward wildfire is unique compared with our responses to other natural disasters. In part, this is due to the ways in which fire is entwined with human history. Unlike tornadoes and floods, fire is not just a mindless adversary, but also a servant of hearth and industry. People use air and water as tools, but not to the extent that we rely on combustion. This longstanding intimacy with flame may be one of the reasons that our response to wildfire is more confrontational than it is to other types of disasters. We prepare for all manner of natural hazards, writing building codes and developing construction techniques to temper the effects of earthquakes, hurricanes, tornadoes, and hail. We fund and build dikes, diversions, and dams to manage flooding (albeit, as is the case for firefighting, with unintended consequences). At a certain point, though, the only appropriate response to these threats is to retreat or take shelter.

Not so with wildfires. Our response to them is offensive, not defensive. A smoke plume sends men and women hoofing it into the woods, ready to engage in hand-to-flame combat. Pilots guide helicopters trailing oversized water buckets and bombers laden with fire retardant. Smokejumpers launch themselves into the ether on the way to smoldering woods. Volunteer crews crank up their hand-me-down trucks.

A disposition toward excluding fires from the woods was part of a tradition of forest management that came to the New World with European settlers. These practices contrasted—and sometimes conflicted—with those of Native American tribes, who used wildfire widely, for everything from range management and hunting to warfare, trail maintenance, and insect control. From the time the U.S. Forest Service was founded in the late 1890s, the agency was motivated to pursue fire suppression in the interest of protecting the timber wealth of the nation's publicly held forests. The most pointed expression of the antifire philosophy was codified in 1935, as the 10 a.m. policy. This protocol set a goal of extinguishing all forest fires by midmorning the day after they were spotted. Although the 10 a.m. policy was set aside in the 1970s in favor of practices intended to allow for the return of more natural fire regimes, a majority of forest fires are still actively fought once they're detected.

This adversarial posture evokes allusions to military combat —territory is won and lost, assaults occur along fronts, heroes emerge—but the links are not merely semantic. The desire to deliver firefighters to roadless areas, for example, spurred the development of the smokejumper program, which predated the use of paratroopers during World War II. After that war, surplus equipment and trained aviators brought a new level of technical sophistication to the fight. The coordination of personnel and resources on large fires relies on command and control structures akin to those the armed forces use. Geographic information systems technology developed for military use also aids firefighters, and troops are occasionally called in to help fight large fires.

And, as in wartime, the public has been called upon to do its part in the fight against forest fires. Artist James Montgomery Flagg used the same allegorical figure he had created for World War I recruitment posters for one of the earliest public service campaigns sponsored by the Forest Service. The image he painted depicts a haggard Uncle Sam pointing at burning woods. The caption reads, "Your forest, your fault, YOUR LOSS." There's a picture of the original paint-ing in Stephen J. Pyne's *Fire in America: A Cultural History of Wildland and Rural Fire*, standing on an easel and flanked by Flagg and Franklin Delano Roosevelt. The image gave me a jolt of recognition when I turned the page in Pyne's hefty tome: a framed copy of the poster hung in our houses throughout my childhood, a souvenir of my father's days working for the Forest Service.

Later, public service campaigns featured softer figures than Flagg's outraged Uncle Sam. I had less regular con-tact with Bambi and Smokey Bear, but campaigns featuring these characters shared the same aim: to evoke an emotional response on the part of the public. Uncle Sam played on patriotism and the protection of national assets, while the animal characters went for raw emotion and the soft un-derbelly of the nation's youth. Human-caused fires were the implicit targets, but the more general result was that fire be-came the villain in parables of loss for generations of Ameri-can children.

• • •

The American perception of wildfire, then, mixes natural disasters, preventable calamities, and heinous foes. In the larger scheme of things, however, fire is an ordinary eco-logical event and force for renewal. Wildfires burn away dead vegetation and clear underbrush, and some forest trees, such as lodgepole pine, have coevolved with fire to the ex-tent that it plays a central role in their reproductive cycle. More intense stand-replacing fires open up the tree canopy, allowing tree species such as aspen to take their turn in the slow-moving succession by which the landscape changes its botanical clothing. The ponderosa pines typical of both Fourmile Canyon and the region around Cap Rock evolved in the context of relatively frequent fires burning through the woods once every ten to twenty years. The thick scaly bark of ponderosa trees is an adaptation against low-intensity ground fires, allowing mature trees to withstand flames that thin seedlings and convert the litter of needles to fertilizing ash. The resulting mix of flora is more parklike than a forest canopy in the conventional sense, with widely spaced trees and ample sunlight.

The ecological rationale for letting more fires burn is persuasive, but it runs in to a host of complications. A century's worth of accumulated forest fuels means that fires exhibit more aggressive and unpredictable behavior, particularly in the context of factors associated with global climate change, such as heat, drought, wind, insect infestations, and the early melting of snowpack that extends the fire season earlier into the spring. Reducing the fuel load over millions of acres isn't easy. Prescribed burns are complicated bureaucratic and logistical undertakings that pose the risk of escaped fires, and they're frequently unpopular with the public because of smoke or because they require recreational closures or because people express a distaste for the resulting burned landscapes. Mechanical thinning is expensive, labor-intensive, and criticized by some environmental groups. The timber industry has an obvious interest in not letting the woods burn. Another economic wrinkle is posed by the fact that wildland firefighting has grown into a considerable, albeit largely seasonal, industry. Fighting fires means a paycheck for thousands of workers. Cash-strapped volunteer fire departments may be able to buy a shiny new rig out of the reimbursement money they take in fighting nonlocal fires during a busy season. Dozens of manufacturers make a profit and pay their employees by making and selling specialized firefighting tools, chemicals, equipment, and clothing.

In the fall of 2010, the Fourmile Canyon Fire became the most destructive wildfire in Colorado history, a title previously held by the Hayman Fire, which burned through roughly 138,000 acres and 133 structures in central Colorado in 2002. In the summer of 2012, Colorado was in the midst of another extreme fire season. The High Park Fire west of Fort Collins began on June 9 and burned 257 homes, overtaking the Fourmile Canyon burn for destructiveness. Then, just a few weeks later, the Waldo Canyon Fire blew up into the western suburbs of Colorado Springs and consumed 346 homes on a single night, June 26.

The upward ratcheting of Colorado's "most destructive" statistics is not based on the number of acres of woods burned, but on the number of structures destroyed. Herein lies the biggest factor complicating the issue of wildfire in the United States: we're no longer talking about "forest" fires per se, we're talking about fires that burn in the so-called wildland-urban interface, or WUI. This term refers to wild or wildish landscapes where structures, usually houses, have been built and where the risk of losses due to wildfire are thereby increased. It's inviting to think of the WUI as ex-urban development in western conifer forests, but the WUI also exists in the South, the Southwest, the Midwest, Texas, and California. The hardwood forests of the East and Northeast are less fire-prone, but like western forests they are increasingly densely populated with both trees and people. The fire hazards associated with the WUI make no distinction between working-class neighborhoods and ritzy resorts. The Waldo Canyon Fire prodded Coloradoans to recognize what Californians have long known: that the WUI includes the suburban fringes of major cities.

The acronym WUI is effectively an alternate term for sprawl. From an environmental perspective, the pat answer to the issue, as it usually is when the topic has to do with development, is to just say no: stop building. But even if new home construction halted tomorrow—or if it had been stopped in 2010 in the aftermath of the Fourmile Canyon Fire or, for that matter, in 1994 before the subdivision in which I currently live was approved—millions of homes would still exist in the WUI. The interface zone consists of more than just new subdivisions. Entire small towns exist in the WUI, including historic mining, logging, and agricultural communities. According to Forest Service statistics, 39 percent of all houses in the continental United States lie within the WUI.

As if the rising density of people and buildings in environments evolved to burn weren't challenging enough, human activities add to the list of potential ignition sources. Many wildfires are caused by lightning, but Smokey Bear wasn't entirely out of line with his famous line "Only YOU can prevent forest fires": humans and human activity multiply the ways in which fires get started. Campfires, tossed cigarettes, playing kids, and arson are classics, of course, but to these add vehicles parked in tall grass; sparks thrown by earthmoving equipment, welding, or even horseshoes; recreational shooting; electric fences. Carelessness is a factor in plenty of anthropogenic fires, but some are accidents, pure and simple. A ranch hand who worked in this area for years once told me about a friend who, having hiked to the top of Cap Rock Ridge, lay down for a nap. He woke up to find that the sun shining through his water bottle had been focused as if through a magnifying lens and had set the grass on fire. The slash pile that was the ignition source for the Fourmile Canyon Fire had been burned and doused by a member of the local volunteer fire department.

Fire risks in the WUI reveal another layer of the effects of population growth and the development associated with it. Some of these issues are practical, but they're rooted in thorny philosophical quandaries. Speaking of the WUI requires talking about politics, public lands management, private property rights, personal responsibility, and the concept of home all in one breath. What to do?

· · ·

Back in 2002, as construction on our house north of Cap Rock Ridge was getting under way, lightning ignited a grass fire on one of the slopes northwest of us. Against the backdrop of drought-fueled megafires burning across the West that year, this was a runt, a dink, a pissant: a creeping grass fire that triggered no evacuations and didn't earn a mention on the evening news. Our little fire stayed little, though, because too many fires that summer had already exploded into monsters: fire management agencies weren't leaving many fires to their own devices. With the southern front of the Hayman Fire less than twenty miles away, resources were easily diverted. Slurry bombers began to lumber over our cabin on the way to and from the site not long after local firefighters arrived. Late that evening, Doug and I watched a group of smokejumpers drift to the ground, their profiles black against clouds illuminated by the setting sun.

Our efforts at reducing our property's vulnerability to fire had begun well before that, but the incident reinforced their relevance. Despite its less-than-woodsy character, we had selected stucco siding for the cabin and used it on the house as well. We minimized wood trim and tiled the deck overlooking the wooded slope rather than using wooden decking. We've been careful about how we landscape, seeking low-growing and xeric plants with low ignitability. The woodpile is fifty feet down the hill, and the propane tank is buried. We've undertaken major wildfire mitigation projects, sacrificing mature evergreens to establish defensible space, then cutting back the brush, shrubs, and small trees that could act as ladder fuels for the trees beyond. Mowing, clearing brush, and low-limbing are part of our annual maintenance routine.

The silver lining of catastrophic fire events is that fewer and fewer homeowners in the WUI have plausible deniability regarding the risks inherent to their settings. As more large fires rip through more regions, developers and realtors may begin to promote firewise construction and lot maintenance as benefits that make a property more desirable, rather than pretending that the hazard doesn't exist or downplaying preventative measures for fear of calling attention to a property's less desirable attributes. Boulder County is notorious for its restrictive zoning efforts—either progressive or draconian, depending on your point of view. If new construction is going to be permitted in fire-prone areas, though, building codes that reduce ignitability hazards, mandate mitigation, or require cisterns hardly seem unreasonable. As more fires burn, more counties and municipalities will likely push for such measures, although getting them approved will be a different matter.

Our property was once part of a ranch that encompassed tens of thousands of acres, all of it managed by a single family. The irony of land use patterns in the West today is that the decisions made with regard to smaller and smaller pieces of land have greater and greater repercussions. As thousands of thirty-five-acre (and smaller) lots are carved from what was most recently open range or wild woods, the pressures exerted on small areas are compounded many times over. These pressures are all the more intense given that such land is typically marketed as a retreat from life's burdens. The last thing new owners want to hear is that they need to cut trees or manage their animals' grazing or adjust their dreams of rural living to accommodate wildlife—or wildfire.

The West is burdened by the wishes and desires of a growing population, though, and it's clear that the time has come to expect more of small landowners. Living in the interface entails responsibilities that go with the privileges of proximity to wildlands. Large-scale projects, whether the intent is landscape restoration or wildfire mitigation, are a vital part of the modern stewardship repertoire, but I have to believe that small, individually motivated efforts have their place as well. I've been working for a long time at understanding what my obligations toward the land are. Pulling weeds, regarding pastures as more than pens, and trying out options for wildlife-compatible fencing are tiny steps toward this end. Mitigation cuts a different direction, seeking to protect my own habitat as opposed to that of the local flora and fauna, but in places where fires aren't likely to be tolerated, thinning can help maintain forest diversity and health. Mitigation is also a step toward self-reliance. One of the social consequences of living in the WUI is that outlying residents strain emergency services. Make no mistake, I'm grateful for the service of our local fire department and would be happy to see their trucks rolling in if a fire was approaching. I consider the safety of our home to be primarily the responsibility of Doug and me, however, and I don't think I should expect our volunteer firefighters to act in defense of our property if we have not first bothered to do so ourselves.

· · ·

Mitigation requires making sometimes-major changes to the environment around a house. Having grown up with overgrown woods as our template, most of us perceive dense tree cover as a desirable archetype. Felling trees goes against the spirit of what draws most people to live in wooded areas. Mitigation is hard work to do yourself, and expensive to hire out.

But research indicates that it's effective. Wildfires invite apocalyptic images of towering flames engulfing homes, but wind-borne embers are the most frequent cause of home ignition. The Fourmile Canyon Fire preliminary findings, issued by the Forest Service in October 2011, showed that 139, or 82.7 percent, of the 168 homes that burned were ignited by surface fire. Only 17.3 percent were ignited by crown fire. This means that a majority of the homes probably caught fire because of embers falling onto a deck, or onto pine needles in a gutter, or onto a woodpile stacked against the house. A wooden fence might have served as a wick, leading flames to a garage or exterior wall. A spark might have blown into an unscreened roof vent or open window. Shrubs and tall grass, doormats and rugs, lumber piles, doghouses and trellises: the potential ignition sources are many, but most of them can be eliminated or relocated.

The evidence in favor of mitigation could put a new twist on Smokey Bear's nagging message: "Only YOU can prevent your home from burning down in a wildfire." This tag isn't as pithy as the original, but it could catch on. The connection between personal behavior and potential outcome in this updated slogan is more pointed than the old campaigns that focus only on forests burning. The connection between location and risk is clear, as is the implication that homeowners should bear more of the financial burden of defensive action.

Properly executed, mitigation offers the best chance that we know of for house survival in a wildfire event. Defensible space buys time for firefighters, and in the triage of an approaching fire, those homes with a perimeter that's been thinned are more likely to be deemed worthy of firefighters' efforts.

But mitigation is neither a cure-all nor a guarantee. Doug and I are lucky compared with many suburban homeowners, who won't have the luxury of mitigating hazards up to one hundred feet away from their homes, even if they're inclined to do so. Dense subdivisions are at the mercy of street layouts, landscape design, urban regulations, house spacing and orientation, and the will and financial capacity of neighborhood groups to agree upon and execute measures that may slow the incursion of wildfire and delay house-to-house spread.

The reality with large fires, too, is that there often isn't a big enough workforce to defend the homes that are threatened, particularly in the early hours of a fire. Here again, analysis of the Fourmile Canyon Fire is instructive: 157 of the homes that burned were destroyed during the first twelve hours of the fire, a situation that clearly overwhelmed the two hundred or so firefighters available to work the fire on its initial run. Even when there are enough firefighters for the task, their ability to respond may be limited; aircraft might be grounded by high winds, for example, or crews pulled back for their own safety. Administrative rules, too, may dictate how departments respond. Our local volunteer department is certified for wildland fire only, so while firefighters can try to keep flames or embers from setting a building on fire, they're not authorized to work the blaze as a structure fire.

"Erratic fire behavior" is a term I've come across often over the past few years, and it seems that *erratic* is probably the norm when it comes to wildfire behavior. The idiosyncrasies of local conditions influence fire behavior and growth; once started, wildfires quickly assert a life all their own. The direction and speed of their spread depend on the type, density, and moisture content of fuels, along with terrain and slope and the "red flag" variables of temperature, humidity, and wind velocity. Mitigation might protect our house from wildfire. It might not. There is no exemption from disaster, no freedom from uncertainty, no release from risk.

• • •

Our house is not an investment property or a vacation retreat. It's our full-time residence, the repository of our stuff and our stories. This is the place where we seek comfort, the hearth to which we invite friends and loved ones to share goodwill, a glass of wine, commiseration. This is the home turf we'll defend using all tools at hand, including a chainsaw and a garden hose. Moving here was not a passive act, a whim, or a lark. We moved so we would have space to keep horses and to distance ourselves from certain aspects of urban life, and we were aware of many of the trade-offs we were making. We've spent a decade building and working and watching and setting down roots, both physically and metaphorically. We've changed the place, and it has changed us.

Engagement is not always joyful. I may never be more attuned to my surroundings than I am during fire weather, when the grass has gone brittle, when wildflowers crouch on stunted stems, when the resin of the pines smells like gasoline. I shorten my shower, stop adding salt to the pasta water so that I can carry the water outside once it's cooled and pour it on the thyme and veronica that create a small tribute to green near the front door. Flies, bees, butterflies, and flying ants swarm to the moisture. Long weeks of dry weather make me crabby, restless, jittery. I have a hard time focusing on work. After a thunderstorm, I pace from window to window, taking in the view not for the pleasure of it, but to scan the horizon for gray feathers of smoke. Some days the haze from distant fires erases Pikes Peak and reduces Cap Rock to a ghostly outline. Doug and I sleep poorly, and many nights one of us will get up to pad the window-to-window route, looking for flickers of orange or a glow at the horizon. We stand out on the deck and sniff the dark air for smoke: real or imagined? sharp or diffuse? local or far away? When I go to town, I rush through errands and hurry home as quickly as I can. We cancel travel plans, unwilling to leave home and horses unattended, the perimeter of the horizon unwatched.

Our nice view often includes smoke plumes, some punctuating the horizon like an exclamation point, others swelling into masses that rise high above the mountains and roil with weather generated by the smoke and heat below. The outdoor fire season now seems to stretch from March through November. The past two years have given me ample incentive to think about wildfire, our house, and what to do should the two someday meet. With every front-seat-to-a-fire-plume scare, I make a little more progress toward our emergency plan: organizing documents; figuring out where to take the horses if we need to evacuate them; building one checklist of what to take and what to do as we're leaving if we need to evacuate ourselves, another of what to do if we decide to stay and defend the house.

In addition to the one I've already mentioned, another grass fire burned west of our house site in 2002. This one was stopped at the road, fifty-odd feet away from our property's western boundary. Along with several neighbors, I walked the ashy land in the days following, hunting for hotspots among the blackened stumps of the scrub oak. I would pause to examine rocks split by the flames, to trace the feathery patterns etched on their surfaces by lichen that had burned away. Now, when I find bald rocks bearing similar patterns in parts of the horse pasture, I recognize them as evidence of other fires that have moved across this landscape.

One of these burned on the opposite side of our land, east of the house, thirty years or more ago. The small grove of aspen trees there has trunks gouged and twisted with fire scars. Many of the ponderosa pines also have scars at the bases of their trunks. The thickets of oak brush on the slope below the aspens are stubby. Like wind and drifting snow and rattlesnakes, fires are not an abstraction or a vague statistical probability. They're a regular and unavoidable presence. Like the wildlife, like the grass and the trees, they're a part of my surroundings, part of the life I've chosen.

A Day with Nothing More Urgent than This

At the Bosque del Apache National Wildlife Refuge in south-central New Mexico, the sandhill cranes are not yet awake. It's early February, barely dawn, and a brightening sky throws pewter light over the pond in front of me, its surface rough with ice. Backed by cottonwoods and distant hills, the far side of the pond is still deep in twilight, but I can hear snow geese there, conversing among themselves with a nasal chatter. In the middle of the pond, I can see dark silhouettes against the pale sheen of the ice: the silent rounded humps that are sleeping cranes. The stark form of a cottonwood snag juts out of the pond near them. The angular lines of its upper branches are sketched in deepest black against the opalescent sky; a dark oval on one branch will resolve into a bald eagle as the illumination increases.

The frost on the boards of the observation deck presses its chill up through the bottoms of my boots, and I think of the birds on the pond, standing barelegged in the icy water. The cranes winter here as they have for generations. In a few weeks, they will begin to fly north toward the Canadian plains to breed. They will fly through my home state of Colorado, stopping in fields and wetlands to rest along the way.

A few years ago, Doug and I went to see the migrating cranes at a refuge in the San Luis Valley, near Colorado's southern border. At the edge of a field where grain had been cut and left as forage, we watched the big smoke-colored sandhills fly in for the night. Gliding down with hollow cries, the cranes would alight with a few bouncing steps, and then straighten. Long-necked and long-legged, they arranged the distinctive flounce of feathers at their rear with a few shakes and stalked the ground with deliberate steps, an endearing mix of gawkiness and grace.

The field where my husband and I stood watching was just a couple of miles from a major east-west highway that I traveled uncountable times growing up. Going to visit my grandparents or riding along with my father on business trips, that road had been, I thought, drained of all novelty. Yet here I was, in my thirties, watching a spectacle I had never seen before. I don't know for sure why we never stopped, but I suspect it was mostly the lack of time: to be on the road with my father at the wheel was to be caught up in his singular goal of getting where he was going, as fast as possible.

• • •

Today, at the urging of a friend, I've made time for the cranes. Lisa stands nearby, her Houston-adapted blood gelid in this air, when something startles the geese. There is a whir that grows into the roar of thousands of wings in motion. The birds' cries are layered over the thunderous wingbeats, a shrieking, honking cacophony. The flock ascends, a blur of white flowing toward us out of the gloom. The noise is terrific, a blast of feathers and voices. The geese circle over our heads and then settle again.

In front of us, the sandhills' heads are still tucked beneath their wings; they seem oblivious to the racket. The sun is not yet up, but I can now see them through my binoculars: white frost has settled on their gray backs. They stand in small pools of open water, the skim of ice held at bay by the heat of their bodies or their slight movements in the night.

They will take their time waking. When the sun is fully up, they will straighten their lanky necks to reveal the red crowns on their heads. They will preen and call to one an-other in their comic voices. The geese will burst off the pond all at once, departing for the grain fields in a flurry of noise, their white and black wings creating a scintillating cloud. The cranes will leave gradually, taking off singly or in pairs or in family groups of five or eight or four. The birds, slipping on the ice as they take off, will be awkward for a moment but then will settle into the easy rhythm of their slow and ma-jestic flight. Necks extended, long legs trailing neatly behind, wings flung wide, the feathers at their wings' tips will spread like fingers caressing the air. Lisa and I will look and listen, luxuriating in the gift we have given ourselves: the gift of a day in which there is no place more important than this, no goal more pressing than watching the cranes as they take to the sky.

Return

Years have passed since I've traveled these Utah roads, but the route is ingrained like an instinct and the topography matches my recollections with comforting precision. As the road bends and dips into a shallow canyon, my eyes hungrily seek out the curves of buff sandstone that define the rim of the drainage. I feel starved for slickrock, for landscapes where the greenery of piñon and juniper gives way to a dominance of sandstone. I crave the stripped-bare landscape both for its beauty and for the way it focuses my attention on first principles: water, earth, sky.

Where the road begins to climb the gentle eastern incline of Comb Ridge, petrified dunes undulate into the blue haze of distance on either side. Millennia of fierce weather have simultaneously smoothed the pale stone into sensuous curves and etched the swells with fissures and drainages. The highway follows the slow rise of the land partway up the slope and then plunges into a deep roadcut. Emerging from the perpetual shade of the gash, I take the corner too fast and drift into the oncoming lane. The error is partly due to the fact that I'm peering out the passenger-side window, trying to see the rampart of cliffs that defines the abrupt western edge of the ridge, but it's also a simple miscalculation of the appropriate speed. As the car accelerates down into the broad depths of Comb Wash, I realize that despite my acquaintance with this road, I've never actually driven it myself. Until today, I have always been a passenger.

The first trip would have been in the early 1970s, and I would have been riding in the back of the pickup with my three older brothers and the dog, our boat bouncing on its trailer behind us. This incongruous trip—into the desert with a boat in tow—was destined to be repeated many times over the years, as Lake Powell became a favorite destination for our family camping trips.

Today, I'm making the journey on my own for the first time. About twenty miles beyond Comb Ridge, I turn left off the highway onto the access road for Halls Crossing Marina. As the path of the road breaks free of the low piñon forest and begins a long straight run across sage-covered flats, the contour of red cliffs against the sky to the north clicks neatly into alignment with my memory. At Clay Crossing, I stop for a pee and to admire the outcrop of green and gray soil eroding in artful badlands formations.

I draw in a lungful of the dry air and breathe it out slowly. I feel slightly giddy, a strange mixture of exhilaration and disorientation: it does not seem possible that sights I have not seen in so long look the same as they did years ago. The ubiquity of development in my home state of Colorado has left me unprepared for such continuity, as has the incontrovertible passage of time: it's been more than twenty years—half my lifetime—since I've been out this way. Once I left home after high school I camped with my family less often, replacing such trips with college, travel, and the paired intimacy of marriage. More importantly, I began to explore the desert on foot, without the luxuries afforded by the reservoir. Although I always had vague plans to come back, a trip never came together, and after my father died in 1997 the idea became tainted by loss. I have recently celebrated my fortieth birthday, however, and this trip is my gift to myself: a few days in the slickrock desert for solitary reflection.

Back on the road, which bends and begins to climb at Clay Crossing, I know exactly where to look for the remains of the narrow wagon track carved into the slope by Mormon settlers. A few miles farther along, I effortlessly locate the walls of the little Indian ruin tucked in a south-facing overhang. Then, after driving another ten minutes or so, my eyes and the landscape conspire to jostle a long-forgotten detail into consciousness: with abrupt certainty, I know that the left-hand bend I'm approaching marks the place where I used to eagerly scan the middle distance toward the north, looking for scraps of turquoise blue nestled among the sandstone hills, trying to be the first to holler, "I see the lake!"

Today, there is no blue.

It's true that I've come to this place, in part, to revisit territory from my past, but I'm also drawn by morbid curiosity. It's an April morning in 2005, and after several years of sustained drought, Lake Powell is lower than it has been since the reservoir began to fill in 1963. The delight I feel at being back in the desert and my happy nostalgia of seeing familiar and intact landforms now churn against queasy apprehension at what the reservoir's falling water level might reveal. Driving the last few miles, my heart begins to thump, as if in fright.

As I round the curve where the expanse of Bullfrog Bay used to be revealed to arriving visitors, I'm presented with a vista composed of more sandstone than water. In this scene, familiarity and novelty collide, and I gasp.

These things I know: the form of the horizon, with the angular pile of the Henry Mountains in the western distance; the curved walls of pale sandstone that form graceful cliffs and amphitheaters downstream of the boat ramp; the low-slung stone dunes heaped into a long pink and lavender vista toward the north; the smudge of green cottonwoods across the bay. The sandstone mesas on my right, slab-sided and round-topped like loaves of bread, are as familiar as oft-viewed snapshots.

But the water that used to sprawl across the low basin in front of me is gone. The landforms have reasserted themselves over what I'd always known as a waterscape; what I remember as islands and peninsulas have taken on the authority of mainland. The sheltered cove where the floating marina used to be anchored is a dry bowl. The concrete lane of the boat ramp has been stretched like something from a cartoon, reaching crazily down, down, down for the water's edge.

To my brain, primed by the assurances of well-remembered landscapes on the drive in, the shrunken reservoir is startling. I park in the nearly vacant lot at the top of the ramp and walk slowly, as if to compensate for the frenetic pace of my thoughts. I had decided to drive to Halls Crossing for both practical and sentimental reasons. I am boatless and unwilling to take my aging little car onto the more isolated and remote roads that access the shoreline. More than that, though, I needed to gauge the reservoir's fall in a place that was familiar. We camped in many different places over the years, but for me, almost every trip began and ended here, at Halls Crossing, with this vista.

One of my father's rituals, once he had launched the boat and parked the truck and trailer, was to take off his watch and stow it, along with his wallet, in the wall cabinet of the boat cabin. The wallet sometimes came out to pay for gas or beer, but the watch stayed put: time spent at Lake Powell was time apart. A sanctuary from the day-to-day, this rocky canyon enveloped us in its folds. We hiked, fished, and swam in the reservoir, the water icy during springtime trips, warm as bathwater in the fall. We prepared elaborate meals—crab legs with artichokes, marinated shish-kebabs of venison tenderloin, pancakes and fresh-caught fish for breakfast—and chuckled smugly as we ate, imagining other campers nibbling pathetically on charred hot dogs. We spent afternoons playing cribbage in the shade, talked in the orange circlet of light around the fire when darkness fell. We counted falling stars and watched satellites trace their silent paths through the night. Often, when the bright light of a late-rising moon woke me up, the murmured voices of Dale and Dennis, talking while they waited for catfish to bite, lulled me back to sleep.

I scramble down the rip-rap of boulders at the edge of the parking lot and step onto the slickrock. Striding up a steep incline, I revel in the familiar grip of the gritty stone beneath the soles of my tennis shoes. I descend a bulging formation, stopping just above the point where its curve accelerates to freefall. Violet-green swallows veer below my feet, offering a clear view of the white markings on their backs. I sit down and gaze out over the canyon and its burden of slow-moving water.

The beauty is unconventional. Rather than the verdure of forest or field, the blue-green water laps against stone tinted rose, lavender, and tan. From atop a cliff such as this one, the view is expansive, with stone dune fields, lurid red mesas, and purple mountain ranges punctuating the distance, but I know how it is deep in the canyons' fissures. Down there, one seems to move through, rather than across, the land. Flat water meets vertical cliffs on the perpendicular; in the narrow channels, the sheer walls pull the horizon in close, pinching the visible world down to some fraction of a mile in any direction.

It's convenient to characterize a large body of water in the desert as an oasis, yet here there is none of the lushness one associates with the word. Mapped on paper, Lake Powell squiggles, twists, kinks, loops, and branches in a manner suggestive of organic forms—amoebas, taproots, networks of swollen blood vessels—yet on the ground it is characterized by a dearth of the organic. There are no reedbeds, no marshes, few grassy pockets where animals congregate. Greenery is exceedingly rare: the verdant ribbon that occupied the river channel was drowned when the reservoir began to fill, and new growth along the water's edge is hampered by the harsh desert climate and rapidly fluctuating water levels.

The place is austere, but that is—and was, for me as a young girl—the point. My parents took my brothers and me camping in the mountains from the time we were infants, and a love of the woods feels like part of my genetic makeup, an inborn affection. The sensibility that took root at Lake Powell was a harbinger of the more difficult and changeable love I would aspire to in adulthood: the kind of love I had to work at, the kind of love that demanded changes of me. When I began to think, later in life, about the foundations of my relationship with the natural world, impressions from Lake Powell were always prominent. The barren landscape framed objects and invited contemplation: a circle drawn in sand by wind-spun grass, a lizard doing push-ups, a petroglyph.

Yet the land, in its harshness and verticality, also demanded respect. Romantic notions of beneficent nature evaporated in the kilnlike heat, slipped away with the clatter of a nearby rockfall, were scoured and pitted by blowing sand. The knowledge that Lake Powell was, despite its raw wildness, a reservoir—an artificial oasis—further complicated idyllic reveries about nature and my relationship to it.

I'm thinking about old campsites and what their vistas might look like now when I hear a boat down below. The mechanical buzz of its engine, which I would normally dismiss as noise, is today oddly sweet to my ears. The vessel glides past the base of the cliff marking the far side of the channel. I contemplate the fact that the cliff looming over the boat is at least a hundred feet taller than it would have been at any time I gazed up it from water level.

From where I'm sitting, the change in water level is easy to see; the chalky stains of Lake Powell's high water mark are one of its infamous attributes. The residue invites the inevitable comparison to a bathtub ring, and it baits my eyes into focusing on the water that is gone rather than the desert that is present: the bottom two-thirds of the cliff opposite me is encrusted. The upper portion of the stone face was beyond the reservoir's reach, however, and is thickly streaked with black-brown desert varnish, mineral deposits left by precipitation cascading over the cliff's top. The reservoir hasn't been full in so long that the stains are beginning to over-paint the top of the high water mark.

In my body's sensibility, Halls Crossing is unchanged: same texture to the sandstone, same smell of water and gasoline, same hot sun on my skin, same dry air in my lungs, same sounds of wave-lap and motorboats. This visceral conviction is sharply countered by the visual evidence presented by the shrunken reservoir, as well as the details my mind keeps offering up as gauges of time's passage between then and now: I didn't know they were called violet-green swallows when I was here as a kid, although I did know tamarisk is a weed; I have earned college degrees, lived abroad, become a wage-earner since last I set foot in this part of Utah; have courted and married a man who has never been here.

Eventually, I return to the car and drive toward the once-bustling marina complex. Dozens of rental houseboats are parked in dry dock; the protected basin where they used to be anchored now harbors a graying pile of tumbleweeds. Strips of dock lie off-kilter, grounded by the shrinking reservoir. The parking lots are empty, and their walkways point listlessly toward the distant water.

I climb in the car and leave, but melancholy trails me as I retrace my route out of the canyon, through the stony hills, past the little ruin, down the pass at Clay Crossing. I stop on the flats for a picnic lunch and take a hike. When I originally planned this trip, I had pictured walking as a meditative, contemplative time, but at the moment I am hoping the rhythm of my legs' cadence—right, left, right, left—will calm the tumult of thought and memory that continues to spin through my head.

I understand that tearing out the Glen Canyon Dam would restore the flow of the Colorado River, but my mind fixates on the high water mark, Lake Powell's ghost lingering in the canyon for generations. I imagine a concentrated sludge of algae, silt, oil, and effluent in the bottom of the canyon, along with forty years' worth of dropped and windblown beer cans, ice chests, baseball caps, fishing poles, waterlogged trees and life vests, snarls of fishing line, bait buckets, and food wrappers. Memories flash through my brain like a slide show clicked through too fast: Mom swooping up parallel to the boat as her single water ski throws a curtain of drops, her arm lifting to take up slack in the tow rope. The huge scorpion Dennis found under the cool glass of the gin bottle, a pallid nightmare creature as long as a hand, black stinger a cat's claw. The boat's engine roaring in my ear, its black cover hot under my elbow as I sit in one of the stern seats. My brother Doug building meticulous miniature replicas of Indian ruins in tiny hollows in the sandstone. Dad punching a screwdriver through the head of a catfish, pinning it to a driftwood board so he can fillet it. The jelly bean–sized egg in the grass cup of a hummingbird's nest suspended in an alcove. Cindy's laugh echoing clear and bell-like over Dad's mutters and curses, having beaten him at a game of gin rummy. Jumping in the water after a long hike out of the canyon, coolness closing over my head. Dale quoting Edward Abbey by firelight. Dawn over the canyon after a flash flood, red cliffs hung with dozens of streaming silver waterfalls.

Two hours later, I'm sweaty, tired, and more calm. Back in the car, I arrive at the junction with the highway, and rather than turning right toward the mountains of home, I steer left and head deeper into the desert. This is the road less traveled, and the unfolding panorama is unburdened by memories. I hold the wheel and let the hum of the engine and the monotony of the road's straightaways finish lulling my brain toward a meditative blankness.

• • •

After driving for a while, I see signs for a road offering lake access. I turn and follow the bumpy unpaved track as it winds among buttes and pillars of angular red sandstone. The road descends into a shallow valley, ending at a huge empty parking area. A lonely fee collection station and small hut housing hers and his pit toilets stand at the edge of the gravel flat. I cross the expanse and see a two-track lane leading in the direction where the reservoir should be. I creep my car down a red sand slope and park on a broad flat that would, at some point in the past twenty years, have been under water.

I'm thinking I may try to hike to the water's edge, but this whim is short-lived.

There is no reservoir. There is no sound of lapping water, no hum of distant boat engines, no scent of wet sand or the slightly fishy mustiness of damp silt. The only signs that water has pooled here in any recent epoch is a faint chalkiness on some of the rocks and a fuzz of weeds greening the drainages. The reservoir is gone, and it feels like it has been gone for a long time.

Where the air was pensive at Halls Crossing, the atmosphere here is of abandonment and desolation. I think of the loneliness of ghost towns, but this is more forlorn: there isn't even a town. If I didn't know that Lake Powell's waters once stood here, the expansive parking lot and fee station would seem like a practical joke.

The feel of the place is utterly different from that of the unadulterated desert, where vast geographies, enormous skies, and the harsh climate intimidate but also inspire and invigorate. The desert is not beneficent, but it has a quiet integrity that makes the human presence seem incidental. What is unnerving about this dry cove is the air of *absence*: that the lack of people can be so profoundly felt. The lonely parking lot and weeds and litter of vehicle tracks and trash evoke vacancy so profoundly that my sense of the desert's integrity is overpowered. I wander around a little, increasingly unsettled as the air of loneliness resolves into something more personal.

The confusion of thought and memory from this morning's visit to Halls Crossing rises again, but what comes to the fore is the wistful realization of how much of my emotional attachment to Lake Powell is centered on my family. Camping—that time apart—was our time together. At home, school and work schedules seldom allowed for everyone sitting down for meals at the same time; at home, all three of my older brothers and I played together only occasionally. Our collective experience here forms a distinct storyline in our shared history, but since those days the ties of my family's kinship have frayed and in some cases snapped. Some of the wear has been typical of the evolution of a nuclear family: kids growing up and moving away, spending their time with new companions. Other stresses are more abrupt or more complex—divorce, separation, death, lives grown apart.

Despite my sympathy for the movement to decommission

the Glen Canyon Dam and drain Lake Powell on environmental grounds, my history here has always made me ambivalent about the effort. Lake Powell holds tender memories, and even though my family has scattered, I've held on to the notion that echoes of those times may be found in its narrow passages. In this dry cove, I sense what it would be like if Lake Powell were to disappear, and the emptiness of the place presses into me. Although I grieve the tattered relationships, I am thinking now of my father, the engineer and driver of the family camping custom. A thought finally completes itself, after having lurked as a fragment in the back of my mind all day: I have never before been to Lake Powell without my dad. The loneliness of this place sharpens the blunt fact of his absence to a cutting edge, and I lean on the roof of my car and cry.

And yet the tears don't last long. Abruptly, standing in what once was an arm of that much-loved reservoir, I know I can live without it. My father's been dead more than seven years now. I still miss him, and I wonder how my life would be different if he were still alive, but I have learned to let go of him. I know I can also let go of Lake Powell.

As my sobbing subsides, silence presses in again. I take a few deep breaths, wipe my eyes, blow my nose, and leave.

· · ·

As I approach the turnoff for Hite Marina, I hesitate. I'm exhausted. The day has tipped toward evening. I'm not equipped to camp, and my planned destination for the night is still a fair drive west and north. But I feel like I've come too far to leave this errand—of witnessing? of remembering?—unfinished, so I make the turn. Here, too, the reservoir is gone, but a scattering of campers in the RV park and recently refurbished facilities hold the ghost town atmosphere at bay.

I park and walk to the top of the long concrete incline of the boat ramp. As at the cove down the road, there is no visible water: the ramp peters out into sand. Rather than sorrow, though, I feel growing excitement. What I sense here is not absence but presence: the air is full.

Full of the sound of moving water.

Beyond the boat ramp, a plain of greenery has sprung up. In the distance, from deep within its tangle, I can hear the susurration of the Colorado River. For the first time in my life, I stand in the declivity of Glen Canyon and listen to the river that carved it.

I'm thrilled. I almost laugh out loud. Even though Lake Powell is gone from this place, Glen Canyon and the river that gave it form are present. To my childhood memories, in which the twisting arms and orthogonal planes of Lake Powell seemed uncanny and timeless, I now add this sound, which whispers of the ongoing changes of the planet's rhythms. I suddenly see Lake Powell as a passing phase in the inhumanly long timescale that has shaped—continues to shape—Glen Canyon. The analogy to my childhood experiences is unmistakable: those days at Lake Powell should not be thought of as time apart, but rather as a stage in a life passing through its necessary temporal arc. The legacy of my past here will endure as long as I do. As I stand on the ramp and listen to the distant river, I'm oddly comforted by the knowledge that the transience that defines my life also defines an entity many orders of magnitude larger and longer-lived than me.

It's no longer enough to hear the river—I want to see it. I look doubtfully at the green thicket in the distance, calculating its distance in relation to the impending sunset. On the west side of the canyon, I see a slash in the rock: a road dipping into the tangle. Once again I climb into the car, and once again I head west.

Glancing down as I drive across the bridge over the Colorado River, I see water the color of putty and the consistency of milk: the spring runoff is on. The muddy flow cuts through the green plain I saw from the boat ramp; from this height I see that the verdure sprawls over hundreds of acres. I locate the dirt road angling toward the river and follow it to where some trucks and vans stand parked, each with an empty boat trailer behind it. The trailers are all similar—low-slung and wide—and I realize they are designed to haul river rafts, not motorboats.

I walk toward the riverbank, crossing a patchwork of slickrock outcrops and eroding clumps of silt. I wander among thickets of tamarisk and Russian thistle, realizing that the green plain I saw from the bridge is composed of these weeds. It also occurs to me that I'm standing among the Grand Canyon's missing beaches: the sediments of the upper Colorado that have been settling out of the water as it stalled behind the dam for four decades. The newly reinvigorated river has already cut deeply into the deposits, and I follow a lane that's been bulldozed down the bank to provide a put-in for rafts. The sediment looms thirty feet above me as I approach the river.

At water level for the first time all day, I put my hand in the chilly murk and savor the river's flow over my skin. I feel the ancient walls of the canyon around me, listen to the river churning quietly in its silty bed. As I bend over the water, the sense of repose that the desert offers me at long last settles in.

My hand numbs, and I straighten. There is snow in the mountains, and the Glen Canyon Dam still stands: the river's current will stagnate whenever the reservoir rises again. Eventually, though—perhaps in my lifetime—the Colorado River will rumble through a landscape I've always known as a reservoir. I'll surely never live to see Glen Canyon without the rime of Lake Powell's high water mark, but that, too, will someday vanish, scoured away by wind and painted over by desert varnish.

Later, I'll think about how much harder it will be to restore the health of the watershed than it will be to restore the water's flow: ecosystems so long buried by silt and garbage and the patient seeds of weeds will not rebound quickly. Later, I'll be struck by how much the crumbly sediment of the fresh-cut riverbank resembles the canyon's ancient sandstone walls. Later, I'll think about how the currents of a life sometimes curve back on themselves, reexposing what we thought was gone and reminding us where we've been, what we're made of.

For now, though, I simply linger at the water's edge, watching from deep within Glen Canyon as amber light plays across the river's gray-brown ripples and saturates the colored bands of the sandstone cliffs toward the east. I cannot ignore the silt or the weeds, but I can see them for what they are: features of the canyon at this stage of its existence. They alter the integrity of this desert landscape, but they do not destroy it.

Water. Earth. Sky.

Poised at the boundary of fluid and stone, in this moment between river and reservoir, I am filled.

My Life as a Weed

The silver-gray plant stands out against the tan- and rust-colored needles of dried autumn grasses. More handsome than showy, it hunkers low to the ground, with stems that radiate from a central crown and sprout paired leaves along their arc. The leaves get their silvery sheen from a pelt of fine hairs, and they taper to points like spearheads, as uniform and neat as an art deco illustration. The flowers are gone now, but they would have risen from the center of the plant on straight leafless stems, each bearing a cluster of white blossoms tinged with green, lavender, or pink.

Oxytropis sericea. I admire the plant for a moment as I nudge the point of my shovel against the base of the fountain of stems, tap it downward with my foot, then lever the tool back until I feel the telltale *pop* of a root being severed. I stuff the plant into the empty feed bag next to me and move on, eyes scanning the ground. I see another plant, similar in size and configuration, although its leaves are more green, less silver. This is *Oxytropis lambertii*, which flowers in hues of striking purple-rose. I uproot this plant in the same manner as the other and likewise cram it into the bag.

Oxytropis is a legume, fixing nitrogen in the soil, helping to make the nutrient available to other plants. The species is native to these parts, providing some of our most reliable summer flower displays: in all but the driest years, the grasslands will be flecked with purple and white. I am, nevertheless, spending this pretty fall afternoon digging the plants out, having been forced to recategorize *Oxytropis*, on this particular plot of land, from wildflower to weed.

The common definition of a weed is a plant that's not desired or valued where it's growing, and *Oxytropis* lives unmolested on other parts of our property. Within this fenced enclosure, though, it's undesirable because it's toxic. The common name for *Oxytropis*, locoweed, sounds like something out of a cornball western movie, but the plants are indeed dangerous. They harbor a toxin called swainsonine, which, when consumed in high enough quantities, causes brain damage in animals. Symptoms of locoism range from stumbling movements to nervousness to seizures: craziness. Like most forms of neurological damage, locoism is permanent. Horses are more susceptible than cattle or sheep, and loco horses, if they don't die outright, are usually destroyed, since the combination of clumsiness and erratic behavior makes them dangerous.

Digging these plants out of our horse pasture hardly seems worthy of angst, then, and as if to demonstrate the legitimacy of my chore, my little bay horse wanders over to where I'm working. Moondo noses the bag, toppling it over. I shoo him away, reset the bag, and return to my digging. When I turn back with a handful of wilting locoweed crowns, he's knocked the bag over again and has its bottom seam in his teeth. As I watch, he gives his prize a shake, spilling plants out onto the ground, then drops the bag and stands looking at me, as if waiting for praise for a trick well done.

· · ·

Back before the pasture was fenced and the horses arrived, I asked the old rancher south of us whether I needed to worry about locoweed. He barked a laugh and said I didn't have enough locoweed around to worry about. I valued his judgment but still asked our veterinarian about the risks as well. While he conceded that locoweed is worthy of concern, he didn't think we would have a problem as long as we managed our pastures. Locoism in horses typically develops only after they eat a lot of *Oxytropis*, and the plants aren't very palatable. On overgrazed pastures, however, animals will browse locoweed for lack of anything else to eat, and the conventional wisdom is that the plants induce addiction: once animals consume them, they begin to seek the plants out, even when other food is available. I work at keeping our pastures from getting grazed down too far, fencing off sections if need be, and I've watched our horses eat. They don't seem to have a taste for locoweed, but they could have seasonal preferences I'm not aware of. Swainsonine accumulates in tissues rather than passing through an animal's system; both of our horses were in their teens when we bought them, and I have no way of knowing what their lifetime body burden of swainsonine might be. Its toxicity has been linked to selenium levels in the soil, and my attempts to learn about my home ground have not yet extended to soil chemistry testing. As the uncertainties pile up, action feels preferable to inaction, and the thought of having to put one of our horses down wins out over the guilt I feel about digging up native plants.

The locoweed belongs to the tribe of flora I embrace as part of the distinct beauty and character of this place. Hav-

ing arrived here with aspirations of fitting in, grubbing out
these plants makes me feel like the worst kind of exotic pest,
pushing out the natives. Plants like *Oxytropis* are adapted to
the local climate, soil conditions, and precipitation patterns;
they persist by making good on the genetic wisdom of past
generations. Native plants are grounded not only because
they're anchored in a particular location, but because their
lives are linked to those of pollinators, the soil, and other
plants, bound by flows of nectar, nitrogen, air, and water. Being a native implies interdependence with the local environment, suggests good ecological citizenship.

For plants, behavior, ancestry, and geography are inextri-
cably linked. For humans, the parameters of nativeness are
more complex. We transplant readily. Longstanding invest-
ments in culture and technology mean that we're no longer
bound to our birthplace, by either necessity or inclination.
We balk at the limits imposed by climate, land fertility, or
water availability, and if the place we're in fails to satisfy our
needs or desires, we tend to either move on or set about trying to reshape it to fit.

I grew up in Colorado—was born, in fact, only about seventy miles away from here. From the high ground in this
pasture, I can see Greenhorn Mountain, the same long flat
prominence my grandmother uses to gauge the seasons'
change from her dining room window: "There's snow on The
Greenhorn. Winter's coming."

I am a Colorado native. I know what this means in the
common vernacular of the human community. I'm still trying to figure out what it means for me here, in this community of place.

• • •

I pry another plant from the ground and tamp it into the
bag, which is getting heavy. Letting the shovel drop, I settle
onto the ground for a break. I'm sitting in the wide bowl of

the pasture. Down the slope and beyond the fence line, the basin narrows to a gap flanked by stone outcrops. The late afternoon air is mild and smells of drying grass and sage. The shadows of grass stems, stretched by the low-slung sun, cross-hatch the tawny field around me. The elongated butte of Cap Rock Ridge looms in the middle distance, while the heavily timbered slopes of the Wet Mountains, The Greenhorn's slightly wrinkled bulk at their eastern edge, form a dark fringe on the horizon. The peculiar blend of rolling hills, flat-topped buttes, and wooded north-facing slopes is distinctive and beautiful, and when Doug and I saw this place, we both experienced love at first sight.

As with all romances that mature into long-term love, we've had to come to terms with some of the less charming traits of our beloved, notably, wind and altitude and distance. We've worked hard at adjusting our expectations and lifestyle to fit the realities of our location, rather than trying to force our environment into being, or looking like, something it's not. From the orientation of the house to spacing the strands of fence wire at wildlife-compatible heights, we've tried to take into account and, as much as possible, work with the local conditions. Where we do defy those conditions, we strive to do so with forethought and good reason.

Despite the high elevation, short growing season, and abundant wildlife, for example, we knew we wanted a garden, so we built a walled one, complete with concrete footers to keep out burrowing critters and metal flashing screwed to the top of the wall as a slippery barrier to those that climb. So far (knock on cinderblock), the garden has been unmolested by rabbits, deer, moles, elk, or gophers. Packrats, deer mice, and chipmunks occasionally manage to penetrate the defenses, but for the most part the garden is a sanctuary from any wildlife that does not fly. The wall holds heat, extending the growing season, and it shelters the garden from desiccating winds. The growing beds, covered with mulch and fed by composted kitchen scraps, host a vegetative soiree, with vegetables, herbs, berries, and flowers mixing it up over the course of our short summers.

I still haven't made up my mind whether the walled garden represents an act of accommodation or one of defiance. I recognize it as an imposition of will and desire, but I'm willing to accept its artifice on the grounds that it is organic and occupies a small footprint in terms of both water and space. Certainly, those salads of fresh homegrown spinach and mashes of fresh-dug spuds *taste* adaptive. Perhaps it's a cop-out, but having a small space dedicated to lushness gives me greater conviction in landscaping around the house with an emphasis on tough, native, or xeric plants that can survive up here without heroic interventions—including a number of *Oxytropis* that came up out of the pasture with enough of their root system intact to transplant.

. . .

Both horses have grazed their way toward me and are lurking nearby. They know their evening grain won't appear as long as I'm out here. As I sit looking over the placid view, I consider the notion of human weediness as it relates to my situation. Despite a profound love of the land, despite good intentions and family history and a smattering of salvaged plants, my bag of wilting locoweed still makes me feel more invasive than native.

Some people would say without equivocation that I am, indeed, a weed, neither desirable nor of value in this place. The more extreme view is that the human race has become so irredeemably noxious that we cannot help but disrupt natural ecosystems by living in them, and that the proper habitat for people these days is in towns or cities. The suggestion that humanity is a scourge to nature and that we should, in a gesture of grand environmental accountability, confine ourselves to the equivalent of my walled garden has a dramatic ring, but I'm troubled by the insinuation that if we cannot live on the land with perfect benignity, we should not live on it at all. The notion perpetuates the modern tendency to think of people as distinct from the natural world, but it also infers that we are universally destructive, incapable of self-restraint or restorative action. The implication that people cannot change is surely more insidious than hype suggesting we don't have to.

Another problem with the people-off-the-land proposition is that it places the emphasis on *where* we live, deflecting attention from the fundamentals of how many of us there are and how we live. We talk of sprawl and development as proxies to avoid talking about human population density: the sheer numbers of us seeking places to live. *How* we live is another matter, one of choice and restraint. Weedy behavior is weedy behavior, regardless of where it transpires.

Ranchland subdivisions such as the one I live in introduce roads, fencing, hobby livestock, dogs, cats, machinery, and human activities that stress wildlife and disrupt botanical communities. One of the distinctive attributes of living in such places is that the effects of individual choice are evident. These days, individual landowners—not just industry and not just government agencies—are capable of large-scale alterations to the environment. All it takes is a backpack sprayer of weed killer, a small herd of horses or llamas, a rented backhoe.

The "footprint" issues of our day, from sprawl to water use to carbon emissions, are new twists on the ancient biological truism that life exists by taking other lives. These are the blunt terms of living in a world of finite resources, and these terms have always been in effect, even if our consumer economies have tried to persuade us to ignore them. As an

American, I'm a member of a society exhibiting a rapacious appetite for *stuff*, a participant in a culture that celebrates personal and property rights while downplaying responsibility, mutual obligation, and restraint. The fact that the question of whether or not I should be living in this place can be posed as a matter of serious debate is indicative of the watershed moment in which we find ourselves. Such questions reflect a widening recognition of diverse environmental pressures and reveal a deepening awareness of how personal choices contribute to those pressures. In a city, the choices are different and the burdens—of water use, of garbage disposal, of transportation and food distribution—are more diffuse, shared across hundreds or thousands or hundreds of thousands of households. For Doug and me, the line from cause to effect is, in many cases, direct and unequivocal. My wanderings and wonderings are my way of trying to understand what my presence means in the context of the ecosystems I've recently joined.

I see little value in the idea that people should not live in the country, but I believe that those who do move to less developed locations should come to the decision consciously and with an effort to anticipate the negatives as well as the positives. We chose to live here rather than someplace else because the location offered us qualities relevant to our preferences and lifestyle. We favor seclusion over nightlife, rank open spaces above restaurants and museums. In our free time, we are content to putter on projects, to walk or hike or go for a horseback ride, to drink a glass of wine on the deck. We don't have children and so needn't demand access to schools and youth activities.

I reject the premise that my name on the title to this property gives me the right to do whatever I want with the land, and I disagree with anyone who views the unbuilt landscape as a blank slate, as a canvas for their desires. In real estate terms, undeveloped land is marketed as "vacant," a misnomer that ignores the wild communities that occupy the landscape. When the wild denizens are acknowledged, it tends to be the charismatic species such as elk and bighorn sheep and golden eagles that earn a mention, as opposed to rattlesnakes, mountain lions, bears, weird insects, and rodents that are capable of destructiveness far out of proportion to their size. I don't always get along with my nonhuman neighbors, and I don't delude myself that the "improvements" we have built on this "vacant" land are a net gain for the local environment. But as a matter of pragmatism and as a stay against despair, I must believe that, just as the impacts of my existence are incremental, so too are the opportunities for restraint and thoughtful choice.

By virtue of the location of my birth and the allegiance of my psyche, I am a native of Colorado. This background impels me to favor mountainous places and view water as precious; it lends me a degree of equanimity about fire and erratic weather, most of the time. Still, the process of becoming more native than weed is ongoing. Sitting here with my bag of dead native plants, feeling my weedy worst, it occurs to me that perhaps this is the best I can hope to be in the context of my life here, given my species and the era of my birth. My immediate and palpable impacts this afternoon—each plant popped viscerally from its ancestral ground—heighten my awareness of the costs my choices impose on the world and compel me to reflect on the path that has led me to this task. I dislike my chore, but I've come to it having weighed risk and responsibility, need and desire, local conditions and the larger picture.

I pry plants from the ground. I give myself permission to pick extravagant bouquets of locoweed flowers from the pasture so the plants will not set seed. I nurture the transplants in the flowerbed. Each act is intimate, a direct negotiation between me and a species native to my home ground. I'm not always comfortable with the outcomes of my interactions, but I prize the affiliation.

And I take comfort in the knowledge that my chore this afternoon has been—as it always will be—an exercise in mitigation, not eradication. No matter how rooted I might feel, I am a transient presence here. *Oxytropis* is more elementally anchored. The plants that I admire in some locations and uproot from others are representatives of a long family line. Their seeds can remain viable for fifty years or more, which means that some wet summer after I'm no longer here, seeds dropped last year by one of the plants I dug this afternoon may sprout. The seedling will form its spray of stems and fuzzy lanceolate leaves, will mature to unfurl pale flowers along upright stalks. Petals will unfold and invite pollinators into their origami folds, initiating an ancient rite of exchange that will seal a promise to the next generation.

I lunge to my feet and dust off the seat of my jeans. The horses are alert, watching me. I grab the heavy bag in my right hand and swing the shovel in my left like a walking stick as I begin to angle my way back up the slope. The horses turn to follow, and the three of us amble toward home.

ACKNOWLEDGMENTS

Some of the essays in this collection were originally published elsewhere and have been revised for publication in this book.

"Voyeur": *Snowy Egret*, Autumn 2002.

"First Signs": *Christian Science Monitor*, April 5, 1999 (http://www.CSMonitor.com), under the title "Spring Ascends the Rocky Mountains."

"Where Does Your Garden Grow?": *Christian Science Monitor*, July 6, 2001 (http://www.CSMonitor.com), under the title "City Ways Nurture a Country Garden."

"Love Letter to a Sewage Lagoon": *Camas: The Nature of the West*, Spring 2005.

Portions of "Weed Duty": *In the Mist*, vol. 1, 2008 (online journal; no longer available), under the title "Pulling Weed Duty."

"Picking Up the Unexpected": *Christian Science Monitor*, October 25, 2004 (http://www.CSMonitor.com), under the title "A Portrait of the Potency of What Matters Most."

"A Day with Nothing More Urgent than This": *Christian Science Monitor*, March 1, 2004 (http://www.CSMonitor.com).

"Return": *Wildbranch: An Anthology of Nature, Environmental, and Place-Based Writing*, ed. Florence Caplow and Susan A. Cohen (University of Utah Press, 2010).